Greek Inscriptions

Cover   Votive offering for the cure of a leg. Roman period. BM GR 1867.5–8.117.
(See also p. 21.)

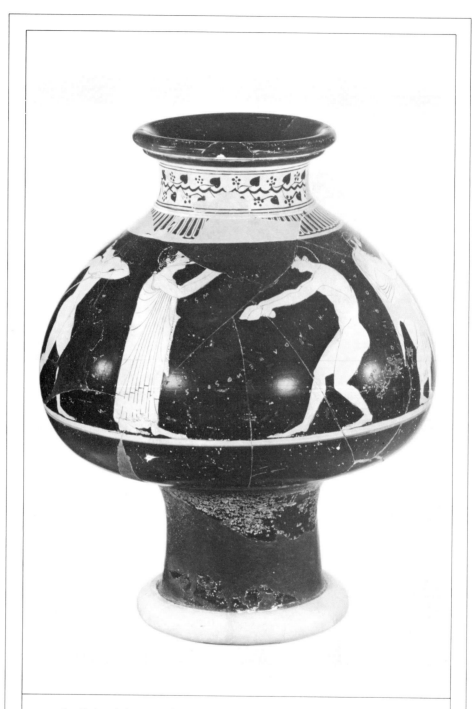

1 Psykter (wine cooler) attributed to Oltos, made in Athens *c.* 520–510 BC.
MMA 10.210.18.

Greek Inscriptions

B. F. Cook

Published for the Trustees of the British Museum
by British Museum Publications

Preface

This book is intended to make accessible to the non-specialised reader some idea of what epigraphers do, and why and how they do it. It is not a systematic textbook of Greek epigraphy, although it may be useful in various ways to beginners in the subject. In order to make any progress, serious students will need at least a working knowledge of Greek and also of Latin, which is still used for commentaries in more learned publications. Here translations have been provided, and the inscriptions have been arranged not according to traditional classifications nor in regional or chronological sequences. Instead they have been divided into two main groups – first inscriptions cut in stone, then those written on other materials – and within each group they have been arranged roughly in order of increasing difficulty, with examples consisting wholly or largely of names at the beginning and those with problems of script or dialect at the end.

The author's thanks are due to Professor Stephen G. Miller, Director of the American School of Classical Studies at Athens, for permission to reproduce fig. 2; and to the Metropolitan Museum of Art for figs 1, 4, 10, 29, 30, 48 and 54 (Rogers Fund), 45, 47, 51 (Fletcher Fund), 40 (Museum Purchase), 53 (Purchase, Joseph Pulitzer Bequest) and 9 (Hewitt Fund, Munsey Fund and Anonymous Gift).

The book has benefited from the general advice of David Lewis and Ronald Stroud, and in particular from being read by Alan Johnston and Judith Swaddling, all of whom the author thanks warmly; any remaining faults are his responsibility. Thanks are also due to Joan Mertens for facilitating study of the inscriptions in New York; to Sue Bird for facsimiles of inscriptions and the artwork for the special Greek font; to Marian Vian for typing the manuscript; and to the author's wife for much patience and support during evenings and weekends.

The author would never have been in a position to write this book had he not received, more than thirty years previously, much kind guidance and help from the then Hulme Professor of Greek in the University of Manchester. The book is therefore dedicated, with affection and gratitude,

TO
H. D. WESTLAKE

© 1987 The Trustees of the British Museum
Published by British Museum Publications Ltd
46 Bloomsbury Street, London WC1B 3QQ

Designed by Arthur Lockwood
Front cover design by Grahame Dudley

Set in Scantext Times
by Unicus Graphics Ltd, Horsham,
and printed at The Bath Press, Avon

British Library Cataloguing in Publication Data

Cook, B. F.
  Greek inscriptions. — (Reading the past)
  1. Inscriptions, Greek
  I. Title II. Series
  481'.7   CN350

ISBN 0-7141-8064-5

Contents

1
Introduction to Greek Inscriptions

The use of inscriptions in antiquity

Literacy, the ability to read and write, has long been one of the hallmarks of civilisation. The lack of writing deprives men of the ability to keep records not only for immediate use but also for posterity. In studying and interpreting the past the absence of records leaves the historian helpless: the prehistorian has to rely for his evidence on excavation. Fortunately the Greeks were literate from a fairly early stage in their development, so that only the earliest Greek culture belongs to the prehistoric period.

In ancient Greece inscriptions on stone slabs and bronze plaques served many purposes for which today we would use printed documents. They were particularly important for spreading and recording information in the Greek democracies, where all citizens were entitled to play an active part in government. In Athens, where the democratic form of government was particularly highly developed, there was a corresponding need for extensive public records, and inscriptions carved on stone slabs have survived in considerable quantity. These include laws, decrees passed by the Assembly, treaties with other cities, war memorials, lists of objects dedicated in temples, lists of the names of Archons and the winners of competitions, records of the sale at auction of confiscated property, and the accounts of income and expenditure of public funds. Similar inscriptions on stone are known from many other Greek cities, but they are not so numerous as those from Athens.

Even in Athens it was not the custom to record everything on stone. Temporary notices like drafts of proposed legislation and lists of men required for military service were written on whitened boards and displayed in the Agora, or Civic Centre. Other records were kept on papyrus and stored in the Metroon, the sanctuary of the

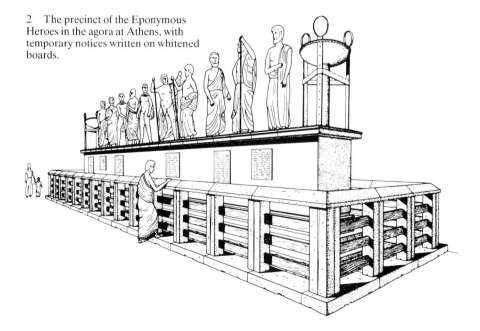

2   The precinct of the Eponymous Heroes in the agora at Athens, with temporary notices written on whitened boards.

Mother of the Gods. This stood next to the Council Chamber in the Agora and so was conveniently placed to serve as a public record office.

Athens was fortunate enough to have quarries of high-quality white marble close at hand. This was used not only for inscriptions but also for sculpture and eventually even for whole buildings like the Parthenon. In some other cities, where there was no local supply of suitable marble, inscriptions were cut on bronze plaques, often provided with holes to make it easy to nail them up in some public place. The long-lasting quality of bronze was almost proverbial, and the Roman poet Horace was to describe his own verse as 'a monument more permanent than bronze'.

Inscriptions were also used by private citizens, for example, to mark their property and especially to make dedications to the gods. Potters and vase-painters sometimes signed their vases or gave the names of the mythological figures they portrayed. The Greeks also preserved the memory of the dead, as we do, by inscriptions on tombstones (epitaphs).

Why study Greek inscriptions?

Inscriptions can be very useful in the study of ancient history, for they are original documents, contemporary with the events that they record, and they tell us many things that we cannot learn from other sources. Some inscriptions provide valuable information about events that the ancient historians described only briefly. Thucydides, writing in the fifth century BC, gives a short account of events between the Persian invasion of 480–79 BC and the outbreak of war between Athens and Sparta in 431. One of the most important things that happened in this period was the foundation of a league of independent states in alliance with the Athenians against the Persians, and its gradual transformation into an empire ruled by Athens. Thucydides describes the process only briefly, and many details of the story are now known only from inscriptions.

The allies all contributed to the resources of the League, some by providing ships and crews for the fleet, others substituting payments in cash. After 454, when the Treasury of the League was transferred from Delos to Athens, one sixtieth of the annual payments was made over to Athena and the amounts were recorded on marble slabs, many fragments of which still survive. Intensive study of the accounts and related inscriptions has yielded much information about the composition of the League and the means employed by the Athenians to gain domination of it. Most of the surviving fragments of the Tribute lists, as they are called, are preserved in the Epigraphic Museum in Athens, but a small fragment in the British Museum records part of the payments in the year 448/7 BC.

Many events were not recorded by the ancient historians, at least not in those texts that have survived, and our knowledge of them is entirely derived from inscriptions. Such events include the treaties made in 433/2 BC between Athens and two Greek cities in Italy, Rhegion and Leontini, and between the Eleans and the Heraeans about 500 BC.

3

5
58

3   Fragment of the Athenian tribute-lists, 448/7 BC.
BM GR 1863.5–16.1.

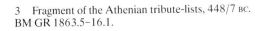

Inscriptions also provide details of public administration or social life that the ancient historians could omit because their readers were already familiar with them. The preambles of Athenian decrees include details of procedure in the assembly, and the methods used to administer public funds can be seen in accounts of income and expenditure and in the records of the stewards of the Treasury of Athena.

In other cities lists of magistrates reveal their precise titles, which varied from place to place. In Thessalonika the title Politarchs ('Rulers of the citizens') corresponded to the Archons ('Rulers') of Athens; in Rhegion the magistrates were still using the Greek title Prytanis ('President') when as individuals they had adopted Roman names after the city came under Roman rule in the first century BC.

			Ionia	Athens	Corinth	Argos	Euboea (cf. Etruscan)
A	α	a	AA	AA	AA	AA	AA
B	β	b	B	B	⎍	Ϲ	B
Γ	γ	g	Γ	Λ	C<	ΓΛ	<C
Δ	δ	d	Δ	Δ	Δ	D	Dᗡ
E	ε	e	ᴙE	ᴙE	B	ᴙE	ᴙE
F	ϝ	w	—	ᴚ	ᴚ	ᴚF	ᴚ
Z	ζ	z	I	I	I	I	I
H	η	ē	⊟H	—	—	—	—
	[h]	h	—	⊟H	⊟H	⊟H	⊟H
Θ	θ	th	⊗⊕⊙	⊗⊕⊙	⊗⊕⊙	⊗⊕⊙	⊗⊕⊙
I	ι	i	I	I	ξ	I	I
K	κ	k	K	K	K	K	K
Λ	λ	l	ᒐΛ	Ⴑ	ᒐΛ	Ͱ	Ⴑ
M	μ	m	ᛙM	ᛙM	ᛙM	ᛙM	ᛙᛙM
N	ν	n	ᛀN	ᛀN	ᛀN	ᛀN	ᛀN
Ξ	ξ	x	Ɨ	(XS)	Ɨ	ƗHH	X
O	ο	o	O	O	O	O	O
Π	π	p	Γ	Γ	Γ	Γ	ΓΓ
Ϻ	—	s	—	—	M	M	M(?)
Ϙ	ρ	q	Ϙ	Ϙ	Ϙ	Ϙ	Ϙ
Π	ρ	r	PD	PR	PR	PR	P
Σ	σ ς	s	ξ	ς	—	ξ	ς
T	τ	t	T	T	T	T	T
Y	υ	u	VY	ᚒYV	ᚒYV	ᚒYV	ᚒYV
Φ	φ	ph	Φ	Φⵔ	Φⵔ	Φⵔ	Φⵔ
X	χ	kh	X	X	X	X	YV
Ψ	ψ	ps	YᚠV	(ΦS)	YV	V	(ΦS)
Ω	ω	ō	ᑎΩ	—	—	—	—

Table 1.   Some archaic alphabets

Origin and development of the Greek alphabet

The Greeks themselves told various stories about the origin of writing. The historian Herodotus, who lived in the latter part of the fifth century BC, records a tradition that the Greeks learnt to write from the Phoenicians, although he was probably wrong, as we shall see, to suggest that it was from a group of Phoenicians who had settled in Boeotia. The Greeks did, however, call letters *phoinikeia* ('Phoenician things'), as he says, and the derivation of Greek letters from Phoenician is confirmed by similarities in their names, by the way in which they were written, and by their order from *alpha* to *tau*.

As Herodotus himself was aware, the Greeks made some changes in the pronunciation and form of the letters. The Phoenicians had used ordinary words for the names of the letters, and the shapes of the letters themselves recalled the meanings of the words: *aleph* means 'ox', *beth* means 'house', and so on. When the Greeks took over the Phoenician script, they learnt the names of the letters by rote. In a different language the meanings of the names were inevitably lost, and the pronunciation was changed slightly. *Aleph* and *beth* became *alpha* and *beta*: the combination of the names for these first two letters gives the word 'alphabet'.

The Greeks found that their language required fewer consonants than Phoenician, in particular fewer sibilants, and they adapted some Phoenician consonants for use as vowels, which were unwritten in Phoenician, as in other Semitic languages like Hebrew. They also invented new signs for *upsilon* and for the double consonants *phi*, *chi* and *psi*, adding them at the end after *tau*.

As the Phoenician letters were adapted to fit the various dialects spoken in different parts of Greece, a number of local variations on the alphabet arose. All of them, however, perpetuated the same mistake with regard to the Phoenician sibilants. The Greek letters kept the same place in the sequence as the Phoenician signs from which they were derived, but each acquired the same wrong name. Thus the Phoenician *zayin* (I) acquired the Greek name *zeta*, derived from *tsade*, and gave its own name to the Greek *san* (M), which took a sign derived from *tsade* (M̌); and the Phoenician sign *samekh* (Ŧ) was written as Ξ and called *xi* in Greek (the name coming from *shin*), while its name was altered to *sigma*, which in turn borrowed *shin*'s zig-zag sign, tilting it from w to ξ or ς. Most local Greek alphabets used either *sigma* or *san* but not both. The uniformity in the errors with the names of the Phoenician sibilants suggests a common origin for all Greek alphabets. Where and when the original Greek alphabet came into existence remains uncertain, but there are some clues.

The earliest Greek inscriptions yet known are scratched on pottery. They can be dated about 730 BC, but it is likely that the Greeks were already writing a generation or two earlier, perhaps on more perishable materials like leather or wood. Some of the earliest inscriptions come from Euboea, and it can hardly be a coincidence that the Euboean pottery of around 800 BC is among the earliest found at the Greek trading-post of Al Mina on the north Syrian coast. Indeed, as recent (1981–3) excavations at Lefkandi in Euboea have shown, luxury goods from the East reached Euboea in the tenth century BC, when the rest of Greece is still believed to have been isolated from foreign contacts.

Clues about the place where the Greeks learnt to write can be gleaned from variations in the local alphabets in use in various cities around the Aegean, especially in the writing of composite letters representing consonants, when different sound-values may be allocated to the same character. Most local alphabets fall into two types, known for convenience as 'red' and 'blue'. In the 'blue' alphabets Y stands for 'ps', 'kh' is represented by X and 'ks' by Ξ. In the 'red' alphabets, however, Y stands for 'kh' and X (or +) may be transferred to 'ks'; in the absence of a single character for 'ps' two letters are used, usually φς but sometimes Γς, depending on local pronunciation. There is a further clue in the use of sibilants, for some early alphabets used *san* (M) for 's' rather than *sigma* (ξ, ς), which later became universal. Thus local forms of the alphabet appear to fall into cohesive groups that reflect the distribution of dialects and likely trade routes across the Aegean.

The Euboeans, for example, who were Ionian, have a 'red' alphabet and use *sigma*. The same is true of the Boeotians and several other Doric-speaking communities in central Greece, and also of various parts of the Peloponnese including the eastern Argolid, Arcadia and Elis as well as Sparta and her Italian colony Taras (modern Taranto). A similar alphabet seems to connect Rhodes with the Sicilian colonies Gela and Acragas (Agrigento). Achaea, however, in the northern Peloponnese, and Epirus in north-western Greece combine a 'red' alphabet with *san* instead of *sigma*. Doric-speaking Corinth and Argos also use *san* but with a 'blue' alphabet. Megara passed on its 'blue' alphabet with *sigma* to Byzantium. In Athens and Aegina, where a dialect akin to Dorian was spoken, X represents *chi* as in the 'blue' alphabets, but *psi* is at first written as ΦS and 'ks' as XS. Surviving inscriptions suggest that literacy came to Athens early. This may account for the initial absence there of the composite characters, which were perhaps invented only after the Greek alphabet began to develop variations in different areas.

Although certainty is not possible since the evidence is incomplete, it seems likely that the Greeks learnt the alphabet from the Phoenicians before 750 BC in a single place, probably in northern Syria, and that literacy spread along the trade routes to various parts of Greece, reaching Euboea and Athens early. Some scholars, especially experts in the ancient Semitic languages, doubt these conjectures and in particular favour an earlier date.

Local variations in the forms and meanings of the characters lasted for centuries, but eventually the Ionic alphabet prevailed. An early Ionic development was the provision of separate characters for the 'long' and 'short' forms of the vowels 'e' and 'o'. In most local alphabets O was standard for *omicron* ('little O'), and it was the Ionians who first opened the circle at the bottom to produce Ω for *omega* ('big O'). Outside Ionia the Phoenician letter ᄇ (*heth*) was called *heta* by many Greeks. Written as ᄇ and later as H, it was used as an aspirate (h). In Ionia, as in some parts of England, the local dialect did not have an aspirate. The character H was therefore called *eta* and was used as the long form of 'e'.

Among variations in the forms of letters *gamma*, *lamda* and *sigma* deserve special mention. The Athenians, the Euboeans and some others wrote *lamda* as ʌ, but elsewhere the character was inverted to Γ and eventually the form ʌ prevailed. In Athens, however, ʌ was long used for *gamma*, elsewhere usually written Γ but as C in some places, including Euboea. For a long time the Athenians continued to write *sigma* as S with three strokes or 'bars', while in many other places, including Ionia, *sigma* had four bars: Σ. After about 450 BC the four-barred *sigma* gradually came into use in Athens, and in 403/2 the Athenians passed a law to make the use of the Ionian alphabet compulsory in official documents.

The Ionian alphabet eventually superseded all other local alphabets and is still in use in Greece today. At a very early period, however, the Euboeans transmitted their own version of the alphabet to their colonies in Italy. There it was taken over by the Etruscans, again with some modifications to suit the needs of their own language, and was later adopted by the Romans, who spread it around the

4   Etruscan bucchero jug inscribed with the alphabet. 6th century BC. MMA 24.97.21.

non-Greek provinces of the Empire. The differences between modern European and Greek letter-forms can be traced to the use in Italy of the Euboean alphabet, which eventually fell out of use in Greece itself. For example, although the first two letters, A and B, are the same, for the second and third letters we use the Euboean forms C and D, while the alternative forms Γ and Δ have survived in Greece.

Even after the Ionic alphabet became standard a number of variant letter-forms came into use, especially during the Hellenistic and Roman periods. They included a rounded form of *epsilon* (Є), a similar lunate, or moon-shaped, *sigma* (Ϲ), and cursive forms of *mu* (Ϻ) and *omega* (ω).

Some features of Greek inscriptions

Boustrophedon

Like the Phoenicians the Greeks at first wrote from right to left (as is still the practice in Arabic and Hebrew), but they soon began to write from left to right if this was more convenient. Vase-painters sometimes wrote in both directions on the same vase. In some early Greek inscriptions on stone each line begins under the last letter of the previous line and runs in the opposite direction. Even the letters are turned round to face the other way. Since it recalled the method of ploughing a field in alternate furrows up and down, turning the ox-drawn plough at the end of each furrow, this
method of writing was called 'ox-turning', or *boustrophedon*. It may be seen in two 29
early Athenian epitaphs and in the inscription from Sigeion. In the printed text arrows 30
indicate the direction of the lines on the stone. 32

Stoichedon

Many official inscriptions of the Classical period, especially at Athens, were carefully carved on stone slabs with the letters aligned vertically in columns as well as horizontally in lines. Since the letters were arranged almost like soldiers on parade, such inscriptions were said to be written 'in files', or *stoichedon*. The same effect is produced by a typewriter, which allots an equal space to each letter, irrespective of its actual width.

Ligatures

In order to save space in Latin inscriptions the Romans often combined two or more letters, making a single stroke do duty as part of each. This practice was sometimes followed in Greek inscriptions during the Roman period. Many ligatures are used in
the Pontarch inscription – for example, ΗΝ for *HN* in the middle of the ninth line. 23
Earlier in the same line is a ligature of three letters, ΤΗΝ for *THN*, and in the line above four letters are combined, ΗΝWΝ for *HNΩN*, using a straight-lined version of the cursive *omega*.

Numerals

The Greeks used two systems of numerals, the alphabetic and the acrophonic. The
acrophonic or initial-letter system used as numerals the first letters of the Greek 3
words for five, ten, hundred and thousand, either singly or in combination. Thus 5 27
(*pente*) was represented by Π, 10 (*deka*) by Δ, 100 (*hekaton*) by the early aspirate Η, and 1,000 (*khilion*) by Χ. For 50 a tiny *delta* was placed inside the *pi* (𐅄), and for 500 Π and Η were combined to form 𐅅. Units were represented by single strokes, and the numerals were repeated as often as necessary to represent particular numbers. Thus ΔΔΠΙΙΙ is 28 and 𐅅Η𐅄ΔΔΠΙΙΙΙ is 679.

The alphabetic system allocates numerical values to the letters of the alphabet, the units from 1 to 9 being represented by *alpha* to *theta*, the tens to 90 by *iota* to *qoppa*, and the hundreds by *rho* to *sanpi* (ϡ). In printing alphabetic numerals it is customary to distinguish them from ordinary letters, usually by adding a mark like an acute accent ' above the line after numbers up to 999. A similar mark below the line precedes the numbers from 1,000. Thus 522 is represented by $\phi\kappa\beta'$, and 5,522 by $_,\varepsilon\phi\kappa\beta'$.

$\alpha = 1$	$\iota = 10$	$\rho = 100$
$\beta = 2$	$\kappa = 20$	$\sigma = 200$
$\gamma = 3$	$\lambda = 30$	$\tau = 300$
$\delta = 4$	$\mu = 40$	$\upsilon = 400$
$\varepsilon = 5$	$\nu = 50$	$\phi = 500$
$F = 6$	$\xi = 60$	$\chi = 600$
$\zeta = 7$	$o = 70$	$\psi = 700$
$\eta = 8$	$\pi = 80$	$\omega = 800$
$\theta = 9$	$\rho = 90$	$ϡ = 900$

Table 2.   Alphabetic numerals

The use of acrophonic numerals may have begun as early as the seventh century BC, but is best known in Attica from about the middle of the fifth century BC. Like Roman numerals they were only really suitable for recording calculations made with counters, and they are hardly ever seen in inscriptions datable after 100 BC, as the less cumbersome alphabetic numerals gained favour. The alphabetic system was not introduced until the second century BC and survived beyond the Roman period into the Byzantine era.

Dating of inscriptions
The date of an inscription is of primary importance for its interpretation, but it is seldom possible to assign a date that is both accurate and certain. Often it is only possible to suggest a fairly wide bracket, such as 'fourth century BC' or 'Roman imperial period'. Usually the epigrapher must seek out and interpret various kinds of information that point towards a date. Sometimes the date is actually included in the text.

It was the custom in many Greek cities to identify each year by the name of the principal magistrate for that year. In Athens this was the Archon, and the names of successive Archons were listed in inscriptions. These Archon lists, first compiled about 425 BC, are recorded in part by the historians Diodorus and Dionysios of Halicarnassus, and fragments of the slabs themselves survive in Athens. It is therefore often possible to assign an inscription to a particular year if the Archon's name is quoted. When the treaty between Athens and Rhegion was renewed, the first eight lines were recut to give an up-to-date preamble, while the terms of the treaty remained the same. In the new preamble the name of the Archon for that year is given as Apseudes, legible in part at the beginning of the fourth line. Since the Athenian Archons took office on the first day of the month Hekatombaion, which normally fell in July according to our calendar, each Athenian year overlaps two of our years and is therefore designated by a double date. In this way the renewal-date of the treaty with Rhegion is written 433/2 BC, because Apseudes is known to have been Archon from July 433 to July 432 BC. Sometimes, although not in this case, additional evidence dates an event in one year or the other, and it is then conventional to underline the appropriate figure: thus 433/2 would mean the actual date was 432 BC.

5 Fragment of a treaty between Athens and Rhegion, renewed in 433/2 BC, when the upper part was recut; the lower part was cut *c*. 448 BC. BM GR 1816.6–10.206.

Inscriptions may also include the regnal years of kings and emperors, and a series of inscriptions on cinerary urns found at Alexandria can be dated precisely by the regnal years of the Ptolemies. The symbol ∟ stands for the Greek ἔτους, 'in the year...'. Although the particular Ptolemy is not named, some inscriptions in the series can be dated with certainty – for example, because the figure for the year is so large that only one Ptolemy's reign was long enough to accommodate it, or because the day of the month is given according to both the Greek and the Egyptian calendar and only one year has that particular double date.

Other inscriptions can be dated accurately because they refer to events recorded by ancient historians. The inscription on an Etruscan helmet dedicated to Zeus at Olympia tells us that it was captured by the Syracusans at the Battle of Cumae. This battle, which is mentioned by the contemporary poet Pindar and the later historian Diodorus Siculus, was fought in 474 BC, and the inscription must have been put on the helmet soon afterwards. An epitaph in verse commemorating the Athenians who fell in battle at Potidaea was carved on a wall-block from their tomb, which was built at public expense. Since this engagement was described by the historian Thucydides, the inscription can be dated 432 BC.

A less precise but still reliable date can sometimes be derived from references to a historical personage, such as Alexander the Great, or to less famous people whose genealogies and family histories can be reconstructed to some extent from a series of related inscriptions. The study of individuals, or prosopography, is particularly rewarding for cities like Athens, where a great mass of material still survives. About 30,000 Athenian citizens are known by name. Epitaphs of different members of the same family can sometimes be linked to build a family tree extending several generations, but other kinds of inscriptions can yield similar results.

From about 332 BC lists were compiled annually in Athens of youths undergoing military training (*epheboi*). After 305 BC, when this training was no longer compulsory, it gradually became a form of higher education for the rich, including rich foreigners, but the custom of publishing the lists continued into the Roman period. 16 One such list, carved on a marble shield, names Alkamenes as trainer. The same man is known to have held the office of Strategos ('General') in AD 209/10, his father appears on an ephebe list of about AD 160, and his son, who according to the inscription served as assistant on this occasion, himself appears in an ephebe list that belongs to the reign of the Emperor Commodus (AD 180/1-191/2). The inscribed shield can therefore be dated within a few years of AD 200.

An archaeological or historical context can provide at least an indication of a date. If the foundation date of a city is known, it follows that all inscriptions from the site must be later. Similarly, in cases of total or partial destruction of a city the inscriptions must be earlier. Some inscriptions have been found in the wall built by the Athenians on the advice of Themistocles immediately after the expulsion of the Persians: these inscriptions must all antedate the Persian sack of Athens in 480 BC. A similar argu- 3 ment could be applied to all fragments of the inscriptions recording payment to Athena's treasury of a quota from the contributions of the members of the Delian League, even if these inscriptions could not be dated by other methods, since all are later than the transfer of the League's treasury to Athens in 454 BC.

Approximate dates can be assigned to inscriptions that show changes in standard phraseology or the forms of the preambles, if these changes can be identified in inscriptions dated by other means. The forms of names and constitutional arrangements can also provide clues. The use of Roman-style names for officials in an 15 inscription from the Greek city of Rhegion points to a date after the grant of Roman citizenship throughout Italy about 89 BC.

Some inscriptions are associated with buildings or works of art to which dates can be assigned on stylistic grounds. The style of the relief sculpture on the grave-stele of 6 Xanthippos points to a date around 430 BC. The epitaph of Rhoumas is inscribed on 18 a herm that incorporates a portrait-head, the style of which suggests a date between about AD 100 and AD 150. This is consistent with the letter-forms, including the lunate *epsilon* and *sigma*, and the cursive *mu* and *omega*.

Letter-forms alone may in the last resort be used to indicate the date of an inscription, although this method of dating is notoriously unreliable, especially outside Athens after about 400 BC. Even in Athens there are traps for the unwary. Although a decree passed in the Archonship of Euclides (403/2 BC) made the use of the 'Ionic' alphabet compulsory in official documents after that date, Ionic forms had made occasional appearances in official inscriptions earlier, so their presence does not indicate a date after 403/2. The replacement of the Attic three-barred *sigma* by the Ionic four-barred version (ξ) is particularly erratic. In private inscriptions the change to the Ionic alphabet is even less reliable for dating: the Ionic *xi*, for example, already occurs along with the four-barred *sigma* in the epitaph of Xanthippos about 430 BC.

The following changes of letter-forms are fairly reliable: from the third century BC *xi* may be written Ξ instead of Ⱶ; before the third century *alpha* with a broken crossbar (Λ) seldom occurs; during the third and second centuries BC the forms of *sigma*

6 Grave-relief of
Xanthippos, *c.* 430 BC.
BM GR 1805.7–3.183.

and *mu* become rectangular (Σ for ξ and M for M), and in the first centuries BC and AD *pi* changes from Γ to Π. In the Roman period *alpha*, *delta* and *lamda* sometimes acquire elongated forms (A to A, Δ to Δ and Λ to Λ), and rounded forms derived from cursive script become popular for *epsilon* (Є), *mu* (M), *sigma* (C) and *omega* (ω). It is always necessary to remember that while the introduction of new styles of lettering may be dated approximately from inscriptions securely dated by other means the older styles tend to persist: inscriptions are sometimes later than they appear at first sight. Letter styles also vary considerably from place to place, so that changes attested in one place are not reliable for dating inscriptions from another.

The restoration of inscriptions

Very few Greek inscriptions, apart from short texts, have survived complete. Most of the stones on which they are cut have been damaged in some way, by the accidents of time, through deliberate destruction, or by later use for other purposes. An inscribed base honouring a successful athlete from Didyma near Miletus was recut to serve as   21 a building block. The whole of the left side, including the decorative moulding at the top, has been reworked. In consequence the letters at the beginning of each line are damaged and difficult to read. The large slab from Sigeion with duplicate inscriptions   32 in Ionic and Attic dialect and script suffered a more bizarre fate. For many years it served as a bench outside the local church, and the inscription was thought to have special properties since no one could understand it. The sick were brought there and rolled on it in the hope of a miraculous cure. Fortunately travellers from Europe copied the text before the middles of the lines were worn away by this practice, and the restored text is based on these early records.

Various methods are used by editors of inscriptions to indicate the restorations they have made. Certain or probable restorations of letters no longer legible on the stone are placed in square brackets [ ]. Round brackets ( ) are used to complete abbreviations, and in this book they are also used for words that are not present in the Greek text but are needed to complete the sense of the English translation. For example, the inscription translated 'Smikylion (son) of Eualkides' says only 'Smikylion of Eualkides' in the Greek. Brackets of other shapes are also used by epigraphers: angled brackets ⟨ ⟩ to denote letters missing in error, and corrections of the stone-cutter's mistakes; hooked brackets { } for duplicated letters; and double square brackets [[ ]] for letters or words that have been erased. It is one of the first duties of an epigrapher to be scrupulously careful in the use of these conventional signs.

Where a letter that is only partially preserved is ambiguous, that is, where the surviving traces do not make it possible to exclude other interpretations, it is necessary to warn the reader of the printed text by placing a dot underneath. When the missing letters cannot be restored, a dot is placed on the line for each one if the total can be calculated. If the number of missing letters is not known for certain, the gap is indicated by a series of dashes. If there is an actual blank space on the stone, the letter 'v' (for the Latin *vacat*, 'it is empty') is used to denote each uninscribed letter space. A single upright stroke | is used at the start of each new line on the stone if the printed text runs on, without regard to the original arrangement. A pair of strokes ‖ may be used at the start of every fifth line.

Epigraphers have a number of techniques to help in restoring gaps in inscriptions. When an inscription is written *stoichedon*, the exact number of missing letters can be determined by counting those in the line above or in the line below, or by measuring the spacing in the same line. Even when the inscription is not *stoichedon* it is possible to estimate fairly accurately how many letters are missing. Of course, a restoration must never contain too many letters to fit on the stone nor too few to fill the lacuna.

An inscription now in the British Museum may serve as a warning. The slab, which 7 consists of eight lines of verse commemorating a fountain house, was found in the eighteenth century. The text of the inscription was published in 1752, but the slab itself was lost to view before a detailed epigraphic examination could be made. The text is quite well-preserved, apart from a damaged area near the beginning of the first line, where a few letters are missing. This gap proved a standing invitation to editors, and several ingenious restorations were proposed in anthologies of Greek verse published in the eighteenth and nineteenth centuries. After the stone was redis-covered in 1970, it soon became obvious that many of these restorations contained too many letters to fit in the available space on the stone, and when the inscription was republished they were simply rejected as being 'epigraphically impossible'. No scholar, however eminent, could escape the limitations imposed by the stone.

An editor's freedom to suggest restorations is also limited in other ways. Proposed restorations must complete the sense and the grammatical structure of the Greek text; the wording must be appropriate to the period of the original; and account must be taken of the shape and size of the stone itself. The last point is particularly important when dealing with inscriptions so fragmentary that none of the original edges of the slab are preserved. Since marble is of limited strength, the thickness of a fragment will give an indication of the maximum possible width and height of the slab.

7 Metrical inscription from a fountain-house on Lesbos, Roman period, perhaps 2nd century AD. BM GR 1070.9–25.1.

Even very fragmentary texts can sometimes be restored with near certainty if the editor can recognise that the surviving letters form part of a standard word or phrase that occurs in other inscriptions. One of the commonest of such epigraphic formulas is the dedication 'So-and-so dedicated (this)', sometimes adding the name of the god to whom the offering was made. The key word is 'dedicated' (ἀνέθηκε).

On occasion historical evidence helps in the restoration. For example, Herodotus tells us that King Croesus of Lydia paid for some of the columns of the temple of Artemis at Ephesus. When the temple was excavated a number of fragments of 8 column bases were found, each having no more than two or three letters: *BA*, *KP*, *AN*, *ΘHK*, *EN*. Variations in the dimensions of the fragments indicated that they belong to at least three separate column drums, but it is almost certain that all of them

8 Fragments of the columns of the archaic temple of Artemis at Ephesus, dedicated by Croesus between 560 and 546 BC. BM GR 1872.4–5.19.

bore the same inscription: 'King Croesus dedicated (this)' (Βασιλεὺς Κροῖσος
ἀνέθηκεν).

Decrees of the Athenian democracy were frequently inscribed on stone slabs for
public display on the Acropolis or in other parts of the city. The preambles of the
decrees, including the names of that year's Archon and other officials, follow standard formulas that lend themselves to comparison with other inscriptions, so that
detailed and accurate restoration is sometimes possible. For example, only the upper
right-hand corner is preserved of the slab on which the Athenian decree confirming
the treaty with Rhegion in 433/2 BC was inscribed. By a fortunate coincidence a dele-
gation from Leontini was in Athens at the same time, and the preamble of the decree
confirming the treaty with Leontini is so similar to that of the Rhegion decree that it
was probably passed by the same session of the Assembly. Comparison with the
Leontini decree makes it possible to restore the preamble of the Rhegion decree with
some confidence. Little is preserved of the treaty itself except a provision for the
Athenians to take an oath to observe it.

Three features distinguish the preamble from the main text: it is cut in an area
slightly recessed from the face of the slab, there are more letters in each line, and the
lines themselves are closer together. It may therefore be inferred that the slab was
originally inscribed when a treaty was made earlier than 433/2. In that year the treaty
was renewed in the same terms, and while the slab itself was reused for economy the
old preamble was erased and replaced. The new preamble, however, was slightly
longer than the old one, and could be accommodated only by squeezing in an extra
line and by making each line contain more letters. At the end of this recut section ten
spaces were left over, perhaps because the stone-cutter miscalculated, so that there is
a long gap between the first five letters of the proposer's name and the last two, which
began the next line and are now lost. The name Kalli[as] can be restored with
certainty from the Leontini treaty, where it is completely preserved. (The Leontini
treaty too was recut in this way, but there it had been the word 'proposed' that was
divided between the end of the new preamble and the beginning of the old text, and
the gap was equivalent to only two letters.)

Among other inscriptions that show the Athenian democracy at work are financial
records, including not only statements of income and expenditure but also inventories
of the valuable contents of official treasuries, such as the objects in precious metal
dedicated to the goddess Athena and kept in the *pronaos* ('front porch') of the
Parthenon. These were entrusted to commissions of citizens and were subject to audit
when each commission handed over its responsibilities to its successor. The inventories are very repetitive, with each year's acquisitions added at the end of the previous year's list. Even though damage to the various marble slabs has left individual
inscriptions in a fragmentary state, careful comparison of the comissioners' names
and the lists of objects for successive years has made it possible to restore missing
letters and words with considerable accuracy.

Most restorations, however convincing, are doomed to remain untested, but sometimes further fragments of an incomplete restoration come to light, to confirm or con-
found the restorations of previous editors. The dedication on the base of an archaic
sculptured grave-stele from Attica, now in the Metropolitan Museum, may serve as
an example. Of the seven fragments comprising the inscription the first four to come
to light included three that join, while the fourth was a 'floating' fragment. Incomplete
letters could be restored with some confidence from the surrounding traces, but
editors have disagreed on the restoration of the missing parts. Since the epitaph is in
verse, restorations must fit the metrical form as well as complete the sense and the
grammar in the available space.

In the first state John Marshall read the surviving letters correctly and proposed to place the floating fragment in the second line: 9a

μνᾶμα φίλōι Με[γακλεῖ με or ὁ]
πατὲρ ἐπέ[θēκε θα]νόν[τι]
χσὺν δὲ φ…

He was also the first to suggest that *Με* in the first line might be the beginning of the name of Megakles, a member of the wealthy Alcmaeonid family. This suggested reading has been widely but not universally accepted.

Some years later Hiller von Gaertringen proposed to read χσὺν δὲ φ[ίλē μέτēρ] in the third line and suggested a different reading in the second, introducing the name of Onetor: πατὲρ ἐπέ[θēκε]ν 'Ον[έτōρ]. Meanwhile, unknown to Hiller von Gaertringen, another fragment had been added. This confirmed his conjectural φ[ίλē] in the third line and the reading ἐπέθēκε in the second. Various other proposals followed, including an attempt by Gisela Richter to restore the whole verse making Megakles the dedicator and introducing the name of Menon for the dead youth.   9b

μνᾶμα φίλōι Με[γακλες με]
πατὲρ ἐπέθēκε [Μέ]νōν[ι]
χσὺν δὲ φίλē[κεῖται
Φαιναρέτē θυγάτēρ]

Me(gakles), his father, dedicated (me), a memorial to dear Menon; with him (lies buried) dear (Phainarete, the daughter)

When the next two fragments were added it became clear that Hiller von Gaertringen's emendations were correct only in the third line. The second line contains no name: John Marshall had been right from the beginning. The text may now be restored: 9c

μνᾶμα φίλōι με[_ <u>ca. 8</u> _]
πατὲρ ἐπέθēκε θανόντ[ι]
χσὺν δὲ φίλē μέτēρ
1. Με[γακλεῖ με?] is restored by some editors.

The last line remains a problem. Dietrich von Bothmer has proposed the insertion of a sculptor's signature in a metrical form that occurs elsewhere: ἔργον 'Αριστοκλέος ('the work of Aristokles'). Although this completes the elegiac couplet, the comment seems intrusive in a funerary epigram and leaves the word 'mother' hanging without a verb, 'dedicated' being in the singular, not the plural form. Unless more fragments turn up to complete the text, the last line seems likely to remain a mystery.

2
Inscriptions on Stone

Although many Greek inscriptions cannot be read and understood without a working knowledge of the language, a knowledge of the Greek alphabet alone is enough for those inscriptions that consist only of proper names. These can be read simply by substituting English letters for the corresponding Greek letters. Epitaphs, that is, inscriptions on gravestones, often consist only of names. An Athenian gravestone of about 430 BC is inscribed simply with the name Xanthippos (Ξάνθιππος).

The full name of an Athenian citizen consisted of his personal name, his father's name and the name of the *deme* or district in which they were registered. The patronymic, or father's name, is in the genitive case meaning '(son) of ...': Σμικυλίων | Εὐαλκίδου | ἐκ Κεραμέων ('Smikylion, (son) of Eualkides, from Kerameis').

On a marble slab in New York a successful athlete is commemorated by an inscription with illustrations of the prizes he had won. The slab is unfortunately incomplete so the man's name is lost, but he was of the deme of Rhamnous in Attica, and his father's name may be restored as Alexander:

Παναθή - ῎Ισθμια ἐξ ῎Αργους Νέμ[εα]
   ναια   ἀσπίς

[_ _ _ ᾿Αλε]ξάνδρου ῾Ραμνούσιος ἀνη[_ _ _]

Panathenaia   Isthmia   The shield from Argos   Nemea
[... son of Ale]xander of Rhamnous...

The surviving illustrations show a Panathenaic prize amphora, the pine crown from Isthmia, the Argive shield and the crown of wild celery from Nemea. On the left, above the man's name, there would have been an illustration of another prize, perhaps the laurel crown from Delphi or even the crown of wild olive from Olympia.

10   Prizes won by an athlete from Rhamnous. Roman imperial period. MMA 59.11.19.

11   Epitaph of Smikylion, mid-4th century BC. BM GR 1850.7-24.1.

Other types of inscriptions could consist chiefly of names – in particular, dedications to deities. It was a common practice to dedicate offerings either in support of petitions or in thanksgiving for favours granted. Strictly speaking, 'votive' offerings are those made in fulfilment of a vow (Latin *votum*), but the term is also applied to dedications in general, including petitions and thank-offerings. In practice it is often impossible to assign an individual offering to a particular category. Such offerings were frequently made to the deities who were believed to be responsible for curing diseases, particularly Asklepios and Hygieia. Asklepios, the patron of medical centres at Epidauros, Kos and various other places in the Greek world, was believed to have been a human physician who received heroic or divine honours after his death. Hygieia was the personification of Health (her name is the root of the English word 'hygiene').

A marble slab, which was found in the sanctuary of Asklepios on Melos, has a relief showing a leg from just above the knee together with an inscription Ἀσκλη|πιῷ | καὶ | ἡγείᾳ ‖ Τύχη | εὐχαρισ|τήριον ('Tyche (dedicated this) to Asklepios and Hygieia (as a) thank-offering'). The aspirate is represented by two dots over the *upsilon*. Note that the *iotas*, which form part of the case-ending for the dative case, are printed beneath the *omega* and the *alpha* ('subscript'), as they would be in a literary text, since they do not appear on the stone. When the *iota* is cut on the stone, this is indicated by printing it beside the relevant letter ('adscript'), as in no. 9. Tyche had evidently suffered from some kind of leg trouble and presented this slab in thanksgiving for a cure. This practice of dedicating representations of parts of the body that have been healed survives to this day in Greece and other countries of southern Europe. The inscription has modern parallels too: the personal columns of religious newspapers occasionally include items like the following: 'Thanksgiving to St Jude for favours received.'

Alexander the Great made a more imposing dedication to the goddess Athena, an entire temple at Priene in Asia Minor. The first part of his long journey of conquest took him through Asia Minor, where he liberated the Greek cities from Persian rule. The historian Strabo records that Alexander offered to defray the entire cost of rebuilding the Temple of Artemis at Ephesus, which had been burnt down in 356 BC, on condition that the gift should be recorded by an inscription on the Temple. There was a precedent for this since King Croesus had dedicated many of the columns of the previous temple. The Ephesians, however, declined Alexander's offer on the grounds that it was not fitting for one god to dedicate a temple to another. No ancient historian records that Alexander made a similar offer to the people of Priene, but the dedicatory inscription on the temple indicates that the offer was both made and accepted; Βασιλεὺς Ἀλέξανδρος | ἀνέθηκε τὸν ναὸν | Ἀθηναίηι Πολιάδι ('King Alexander dedicated the temple to Athena Polias'). After the temple was excavated in 1869–70 by the Society of Dilettanti, this block and several others from the adjacent wall were removed to London. Immediately below the dedication was inscribed a letter from Alexander granting Priene various privileges including exemption from taxes, while the rest of the wall was used for other records, forming a kind of permanent civic archive.

12   Alexander the Great's dedication of the temple of Athena Polias at Priene, 334 BC.
BM GR 1870.3–20.88.

Inscriptions recording the dedication of buildings could include a list of the officials involved in the construction. An example from Iasos records work on the Council Chamber and the Archeion. The Archeion, the residence or office of the principal Magistrate, was also the place where public records were preserved. It probably stood alongside the Council Chamber like the corresponding record office (the Metroon) at Athens.

οἱ αἱρεθέντες τοῦ τε βουλευτηρίου καὶ τοῦ ἀρχείου ἐπιμεληταὶ
Λύσανδρος Ἀριστοκρίτου, Μενοίτιος Εὐκράτου, Ἱεροκλῆς Ἰάσωνος,
Ἱεροκλῆς Λέοντος, Ἀρκτῖνος Ποσειδίππου, καὶ ὁ ἀρχιτέκτων
Ἀναξαγόρας Ἀπελλικῶντος Ὁμονοίαι καὶ τῶι δήμωι.
The elected commissioners of the Council Chamber and the Archeion Lysandros (son) of Aristokritos, Menoitios (son) of Eukratos, Hierokles (son) of Jason, Hierokles (son) of Leon, Arktinos (son) of Poseidippos, and the architect Anaxagoras (son) of Apellikon (dedicated the buildings) to Concord and the People.

Other inscriptions of Iasos and an account by the Roman historian Livy of relations between King Antiochos and the people of Iasos suggest that political concord was achieved in the city during the second century BC by driving into exile those citizens who favoured alliance with Rome rather than with Antiochos. The city's loyalty to Antiochos was secured by generous gifts, and it is possible that he provided the money that was spent restoring the Council Chamber and the Archeion. These funds were administered by an *ad hoc* commission of five citizens.

An inscription from a Roman arch at Thessalonika consists of the names of those who held public office at the time of its construction:

πολειταρχούντων · Σωσιπάτρου · τοῦ · Κλ[εο]‖πάτρας · καὶ · Λουκίου ·
Ποντίου Σεκούνδο[υ]‖ υἱοῦ · Αὔλου · Ἀονίου · Σαβείνου · Δημητρίου · τ[οῦ]
| Φαύστου · Δημητρίου · τοῦ · Νεικοπόλεως Ζω[ίλου]‖ τοῦ Παρμενίωνος ·
τοῦ καὶ Μενίσκου · Γαΐου · Ἀγιλληΐο[υ]‖ Ποτείτου · ταμίου[·] τῆς πόλε⟨ω⟩ς
Ταύροῦ · τοῦ · Ἀμμίας | τοῦ καὶ Ῥήγλου · γυμνασιαρχοῦντος · Ταύρου τοῦ
Ταύρο[υ]‖ τοῦ καὶ Ῥήγλου.

13   Building-inscription from Iasos, 2nd century BC. BM GR 1872.6–10.43.

14 Woodcut showing the inscription on the Roman arch at Thessalonica before its demolition in 1876. 2nd century AD. BM GR 1877.5–11.1.

> Sosipatros (son) of Kleopatra and Lucius Pontius Secundus, Aulus Avius Sabinus, Demetrios (son) of Faustus, Demetrios (son) of Nikopolis, Zoilos (son) of Parmenion, also known as Meniskos, (and) Gaius Agilleius Potitus as Politarchs, Tauros also known as Reglus (son) of Ammia as City Treasurer, and Tauros also known as Reglus (son) of Tauros as Gymnasiarch.

The date can no longer be given in absolute terms since we do not have the annual list of the principal magistrates, or Politarchs, corresponding to the list of Athenian Archons. The title 'Politarchs' (literally,'rulers of the citizens') was used in several Greek cities and its occurrence at Thessalonika is also known from the Acts of the Apostles (XVII, 6:8). Although St Luke quotes the title correctly, this has disappeared in many English versions of Acts either by attempts to translate the term (Authorised Version: 'rulers of the city') or by vague periphrases (Revised Standard Version:'city authorities').

When the arch was demolished in 1876, a slab containing most of the text was taken to the British Consulate in Thessalonika, and it was presented to the British Museum in 1877 by J. E. Blunt, HM Consul General. The ends of lines three to four were carved on the next slab, which was unfortunately not preserved, but the whole text can be read in a woodcut showing the inscription before demolition.

Two of the Politarchs, Aulus Avius Sabinus and Gaius Agilleius Potitus, together with Lucius Pontius Secundus who was father of another, have Roman names, which have been transliterated into Greek. The names of the other Politarchs are Greek in form. A similar mixture of Latin and Greek names can be seen in an inscription from Rhegion (now Reggio Calabria in southern Italy), which consists of a list of municipal officials and sacrificial assistants. Rhegion was founded as a Greek colony about 720 BC, and Greek continued to be spoken there long after the city came under Roman rule. The illustration shows a 'squeeze', an impression of the inscription made by forcing a sheet of moist, soft paper into the letters with a brush. When the paper has dried it may be removed from the stone, allowing the epigrapher to take away a light-weight and exact copy for study. 15

πρύτανις ἐκ τοῦ · ἰδίου · καὶ · ἄρχων · πεντα|ετηρικὸς · Σέξ(τος) ·
Νουμώνιος Σέξ(του) · υ(ἰὸς) · Ματοῦρος | συνπρυτάνεις · Κ(οῖντος) ·

15 Cult-officials at Rhegion in the Roman period, late 1st century BC or 1st century AD. BM GR 1970.6–2.1.

Ὀρτώριος · Κ(οίντου) · υ(ἱὸς) · Βάλβιλλος · Μ(άρκος) Πετρώ | νιος ·
Μ(άρκου) · υ(ἱὸς) · Πούλχερ · Μ(άρκος) · Κορνήλιος · Μ(άρκου) · υ(ἱὸς) ·
Μαρτιᾶλις ‖ ἱεροσκόποι · Μάνιος · Κορνήλιος · Οὖηρος · Γ(άϊος) Ἀντώνιος
| Θύτης · ἱεροσαλπιστὴς · Γ(άϊος) · Ἰούλιος · Ῥηγῖνος ·
ἱεροκή(ρυξ) | Γ(άϊος) · Καλπούρνιος · Οὖηρος · ἱεροπαρέκτης · Κ(οίντος) ·
Καικίλιος · | Ῥηγῖνος · τ⟨α⟩μίας · Μελίφθογγος · Ματούρου · σπονδαύλης |
Νατᾶλις καπναύγης · Ἑλικὼν Ματούρου μάγιρος Ζώσιμος.

Prytanis-in-chief and Quinquennial Archon, Sextus Numonius Maturus, son of Sextus; Co-prytaneis, Quintus Ortorius Balbillius, son of Quintus, Marcus Petronius Pulcher, son of Marcus, Marcus Cornelius Martialis, son of Marcus. Haruspices, Manius Cornelius Verus, Caius Antonius Thytes; sacrificial trumpeter, Caius Iulius Reginus; sacrificial herald, Caius Calpurnius Verus; priest's attendant, Quintus Caecilius Reginus. Steward, Meliphthongos, (slave) of Maturus; ceremonial piper, Natalis; smoke-observer, Helicon, (slave) of Maturus; cook, Zosimos.

It should be noted that although the inscription is in Greek most of the names are Latin in form. The difference between Latin and Greek names may reflect a distinction between citizens and slaves, especially since the steward appears to be on the staff of the chief official. There is also a clear difference in status between those with religious titles (Haruspex, etc.) and those with municipal office, who add their patronymics. Each of the latter follows the Latin convention. In a Latin inscription the first name would appear as SEX(TUS) NUMONIUS SEX(TI) F(ILIUS) MATURUS.

The heading of a list of youths undergoing military training (epheboi), which was carved on a marble shield about AD 200, includes the name of the trainer (kosmetes) in large letters: Ἀλκαμένους κοσμη|τεύοντος ἔφηβοι ('Epheboi, Alkamenes being trainer'). There is a ligature between eta and beta in 'epheboi'. The names of the epheboi are listed by tribes, beginning as usual with the tribe of Erechtheis. The sign ⌐ is used to mark the start of each new tribe, and a curved line ⌐ indicates that the youth's father's name was the same as his own. Abbreviations are identified by a sign like an acute accent (΄).

Ἐρεχθεΐδος	Tribe of Erechtheis
Αὐρ(ήλιος) Δημήτριος	Aurelius Demetrios
Ἰσίτυχος Ζωπύ(ρου)	Isitychos (son) of Zopyros
Ζώπυρος ⌐	Zopyros (son of Zopyros)
Ζωσιμιανὸς Σοφ	Zosimianus (son) of Soph(...)
Φανίας Μυστικοῦ	Phanias (son) of Mystikos
Ἡρακλείδης ⌐	Herakleides (son of Herakleides)

16　List of Ephebes at
Athens, *c.* AD 200.
BM GR 1805.7–3.232.

The names of the foreigners who had come to Athens to complete their education are given at the bottom under the heading ἐπένγραφοι ('enrolled in addition'), and Alkamenes adds a comment in the fourth column:

ἀντικοσμήτῃ δὲ οὐ|κ ἐχρησάμην διὰ τὸ | ἐν τῷ νόμῳ περὶ τού|του μηδὲν γεγρά‖φθαι ἄλλως τε καὶ | τῷ υἱῷ ἐχρησάμην | εἰς ταύτην τὴν | ἐπιμέλιαν | Μ(άρκῳ) Αὐρηλίῳ ‖ Ἀλκαμένει Λαμ|πτρεῖ.

I did not use a deputy Kosmetes because nothing is written in the law about this, and especially because I used my son M. Aurelius Alkamenes of Lamptrai for this duty.

To read this comment by Alkamenes on the actual stone requires some knowledge of Greek beyond the mere alphabet. The same is true of most inscriptions, including epitaphs that are not confined to the names of the dead. A grave-stele from Smyrna commemorates two men, both of whom were awarded an honorary crown by their fellow citizens. The crowns are shown at the top of the stele and ὁ δῆ|μος ('the People'), is written in each. The men's names follow, in the accusative case instead of the nominative that is more usual on grave reliefs, as if they were quoted from the text of an honorary decree passed by the People:

Δημοκλῆν　　　Δημοκλῆν

Δημοκλήους　　Ἀμφιλόχου

17

The men themselves are represented in low relief, and below are eight lines of verse:

τὸν πινυτὸν κατὰ πάντα καὶ ἔξοχον ἐν πολιήταις
  ἀνέρα, γηραλήου τέρματ᾽ ἔχοντα βίου,
Ἀΐδεω νυχίοιο μέλας ὑπεδέξατο κόλπος,
  εὐσεβέων θ᾽ ὁσίην εὔνασεν ἐς κλισίην.
μνῆμα δ᾽ ἀποφθιμένοιο παρὰ τρηχῆαν ἀταρπὸν
  τοῦτο πάϊς κεδνῆι τεῦξε σὺν εὐνέτιδι.
ξεῖνε, σὺ δ᾽ ἀείσας Δημοκλέος υἱέα χαίρειν
  Δημοκλέα στείχοις ἀβλαβὲς ἴχνος ἔχων.

The man (who was) wise in all things and eminent among the citizens, reaching the end of a long life, the black bosom of gloomy Hades welcomed (him) and laid (him) on the hallowed couch of the pious. This memorial of (one who) perished along a rough path his son set up, together with his wedded wife. Stranger, having bidden farewell to Demokles (son) of Demokles, may you travel with safe footsteps.

18 The epitaph of a man called Rhoummas is also in three lines of verse, carved in a recessed panel on the front of a herm, a rectangular pillar surmounted by a man's head. Herms with the head of Hermes or Dionysos were often placed near doorways or crossroads, but this one may have served as a grave-marker and appears to be a portrait. It was made by cutting down a statue, which had perhaps been broken previously. The legs no longer exist, the arms have been reduced to projections, and the trunk has been squared off. A notch about half-way down his left side shows where the rib cage ended, and there are traces of the buttocks at the back. The shapes of the letters, including a tendency to serifs, the lunate *sigma* and *epsilon*, and the cursive *mu* and *omega*, are consistent with the date between AD 100 and 150 suggested by the style of the sculpture. Only one of the eyes has an engraved circle for the pupil: perhaps Rhoummas was partially blind.

The inscription is again cut without regard for word endings, but the ends of the lines of verse correspond with the ends of the fifth, ninth and fourteenth (last) lines of the text. An ivy wreath is used as a space filler at the end of the fifth line.

Ῥουμμᾶν | ἄνδρα βλέπον|τες ἐν εἰκό|νι μαρμαρο‖παίστῳ |
γνωρίσατε | μεγάλας πί|στεις ἀνύσαν|τα δι᾽ εὐχῆς ‖
οὐκ ἔθανέν | γε θανὼν, | ἀγαθῆς γὰρ | ἐτύγχανε | γνώμης.

Recognise Rhoummas when you look at him in a portrait carved in marble, a man who performed great (deeds of) faith through prayer; dying he did not indeed die, for he came by a good repute.

19 An ivy wreath is also used to separate two lines of verse on another grave stone with a slightly gruesome but moralising tone. A representation of a skeleton is carved in relief below the inscription, which reads:

εἰπεῖν τίς δύναται | σκῆνος λιπόσαρκον | ἀθρήσας
εἴπερ Ὕλας | ἢ Θερσείτης ἦν, ὦ ‖ παροδεῖτα;

Who can say, having looked at a fleshless corpse, whether it was Hylas or Thersites, passer-by?

Hylas was a beautiful youth who set off with Herakles to accompany the Argonauts. He disappeared *en route* for, having been sent off to get water, he was seized by the nymphs on account of his beauty' (Apollodorus 1. 9.19). Thersites on the other hand was 'the ugliest man who went to Troy', according to Homer (*Iliad* 2. 216). The implication of the epigram is that the fair and the ugly were equal in death.

17 *Above and below (detail)* Epitaph of Demokles, 2nd or 1st century BC. BM GR 1772.7–3.2.

18 *Above* Epitaph of Rhoummas, *c.* AD 100–150. BM GR 1948.10–19.1.

19 *Left* Funerary epigram illustrated by a skeleton, Roman period. BM GR 1805.7–3.211.

21 *Above* Honours for the athlete Loukios of Miletus, Roman period.
BM GR 1859.12–26.91.

20 *Left* Epitaph of Avita, Roman period.
BM GR 1805.7–3.187.

22 A curse for the misuse of a tomb at Halicarnassus, 2nd or 3rd century AD.
BM GR 1847.12–20.3.

Death came early to Avita, a child of ten, whose grave relief shows her seated with 20 a scroll on her lap. The object in front of her is probably a reading-stand with another scroll on it. Her pet dog sits behind her chair. Ἀβεῖτα · ζήσασα · ἔτη · ι′ · | μῆνας δύο | χαίρετε ('Avita, having lived 10 years 2 months. Farewell'). Her name was Avita in Latin, transliterated into Greek as Ἀβεῖτα in accordance with the pronunciation of the time. Epitaphs of children, especially in the Roman world, often gave their ages very accurately in terms of years and months, sometimes in days, and even occasionally in hours.

In the Greek cities of Asia Minor it was customary for those who could afford it to have a tomb for themselves and members of their families built during their own lifetime. Many of the inscriptions from such built tombs include a prohibition on un- 22 authorised burial there. The prohibition was sometimes backed by the threat of a fine, or, as in an inscription from Halicarnassus, by a formidable curse.

[τ]ὸ μνημεῖον κατεσκ[εύα]σαν Ἑρμῆς καὶ Θοιοδότη Ἀπολλοδώρου· μὴ ἐξέστω δὲ | ἕτερον τεθῆναι μηδένα, εἰ μὴ Ἑρμην πάπαν καὶ Θοιοδότην καὶ Ἑρμην | τὸ ὄνομα τὸ Ἑρμῆδος θρεπτὸν αὐτῶν εἰ δέ τις ἐπιχειρήσι θεῖναί τινα μηδὲ | γῆ καρποφορήσοιτο αὐτῷ μηδὲ θάλασσα πλωτὴ μηδὲ τέκνων ὄνησ⟨ι⟩ς ‖ μηδὲ βίου κράτησις ἀλλὰ ὠληπανώλη· εἴ τις δὲ ἐπιχειρήσι λίθον ἆραι ἢ λῦ|σαι αὐτό, ἤτω ἐπικατάρατος ταῖς προγεγραμμέναις ἀραῖς, οὐδὲ ἐξέ|στω ἐκχωρῆσαί τινι τὸ μνημῖον· ἐπιμελήσονται δὲ οἱ διακατέχοντες | τὸ οἰκίδιον τὸ ἐξέναντι τοῦ μνημίου.

Hermes and Thoiodote (daughter) of Apollodoros set up the memorial. It is not allowed for anyone else to be buried except Hermes the father and Thoiodote and Hermes their slave (given) the name of Hermes. But if anyone attempts to bury anyone, may the land not be fruitful for him nor the sea navigable, may he have no profit from his children nor a hold on life but may he encounter utter destruction; and if anyone attempts to remove a stone or loosen it, let him be cursed by the curses inscribed above; and it is not allowed to transfer the memorial to anyone; and those who occupy the cottage opposite the tomb shall take care of it.

A very large number of surviving inscriptions both from Athens and elsewhere record the honours awarded to men during their own lifetime for various reasons. These often took the form of decrees passed either by the Council in the name of the entire citizen body or by the Council and People together. At Miletus the Council and People honoured a successful local athlete with an inscription set up in the precinct of 21 Apollo at Didyma where the Didymaean Games were held. The steps of the temple itself served as a grandstand for the races, and they are still covered with the names of spectators.

Ἀγαθῇ Τύχῃ | Λεύκιον Λευκί|ου νικήσαντα | τὰ μεγάλα Διδύ‖μεια, ἀγωνισά|μενον δὲ καὶ Ὀ|λύμπια τὰ ἐν Πεί[[σ]]ῃ περὶ τοῦ στεφά|ϝου,

ἀγωνισάμενον ‖ δὲ καὶ τοὺς ἄλλους | ἅπαντας ἀγῶνας | ἀξιονείκως
ἡ βου|λὴ καὶ ὁ δῆμος.

(With) Good Fortune! The Council and the People (honour) Lucius (son) of Lucius for his victory in the Great Didymaean Games and for having competed for the crown in the Olympic Games at Pisa and for having competed in all the other competitions in a manner worthy of victory.

Even to take part in the Olympic Games, which were controlled by the citizens of Pisa in whose territory Olympia lay, was evidently considered to bring honour to the city from which Lucius came.

A very large number of decrees simply give praise and honour, rather like a modern 'vote of thanks', no more tangible reward being thought necessary. A striking example was found at Tomis (modern Constanţa), which in antiquity was the principal city, or metropolis, of a federation (*koinon*) of Greek cities, including Histria and Odessos. They were all on the west coast of the Black Sea, south of the Danube, and the senior official of the Federation was known as the Pontarch ('ruler of Pontos', that is, of the Black Sea). While it is not certain when the Federation was founded, it is clear from inscriptions found at Tomis that the Romans made use of it as an instrument of imperial rule. The Pontarch also served as Chief Priest in the cult of the emperor and in this capacity he was entitled – and therefore expected – to provide public displays of gladiatorial combats and the slaughter of wild beasts. These spectacular events, although disgusting to modern sensibilities, were highly popular in Rome, and the taste for them was deliberately spread around the cities of the empire to foster the dissemination of Roman culture. The inscription, which dates from the second century, records a decree congratulating Aurelius Priscius Annianus for carrying out the duties of Pontarch and Chief Priest, in particular for not failing to provide displays of gladiators and wild beasts. As often, the Pontarch's wife had served as Chief Priestess and shared her husband's honours. Under Roman influence many adjacent letters in this inscription have been linked as 'ligatures'.

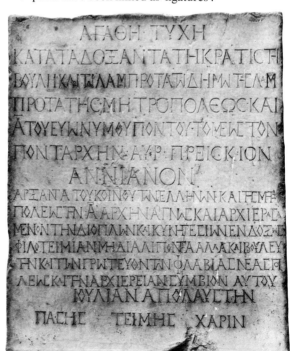

23   Honours for Aur. Priscius Annianus, Pontarch at Tomis, 2nd century AD. BM GR 1864.3–31.6.

Ἀγαθῇ · Τύχῃ
κατὰ τὰ δόξαντα τῇ κρατίστῃ
βουλῇ · καὶ τῷ λαμπροτάτῳ · δήμῳ τῆς λαμ -
προτάτης · μητροπόλεως καὶ
α' · τοῦ εὐωνύμου Πόντου · Τόμεως τὸν
ποντάρχην · Αὐρ(ήλιον) · Πρείσκιον
    Ἀννιανὸν
ἄρξαντα τοῦ κοινοῦ τῶν Ἑλλήνων καὶ τῆς μητρ[ο] -
πόλεως τὴν · α' · ἀρχὴν ἁγνῶς καὶ ἀρχιερασά -
μενον τὴν δι᾽ ὅπλων καὶ κυνηγεσιῶν ἐνδόξως
φιλοτειμίαν μὴ διαλιπόντα, ἀλλὰ καὶ βουλευ -
τὴν καὶ τῶν πρωτευόντων Φλαβίας Νεασπό -
λεως καὶ τὴν ἀρχιέρειαν σύμβιον αὐτοῦ,
    Ἰουλίαν Ἀπολαύστην,
  πάσης τειμῆς χάριν.

With Good Fortune.
In accordance with the decree of the most puissant Council and the most
illustrious People of Tomis, the most illustrious Metropolis and the first (city) on
the west of the Black Sea: All honour to the Pontarch Aur(elius) Priscius
Annianus,
who held with distinction the highest office of the Confederacy of the Hellenes and
of the Metropolis, and who served as Chief Priest, nobly missing no opportunity to
present spectacles of armed men and wild animal hunters, being in addition a
member of the Council and one of the leading citizens of Flavia Neapolis, and to
the Chief Priestess, his wife Julia Apolausta.

After 403/2 BC the Ionic alphabet was used in all official Athenian inscriptions,
including not only those dealing with the government of the city as a whole but also
those relating to individual demes, which had a corporate life of their own. The office
of Demarch ('ruler of the deme') was very important locally, and the Demarch's name
therefore appears alongside that of the Archon in an inscription of the deme of   24
Piraeus publishing the regulations governing the lease of public land to private individuals. Provision was made to guarantee the payment of rents, restrictions were
placed on the removal of soil and timber, and cultivation was forbidden during the
last six months of a ten-year lease to allow the next leaseholder to plough immediately. The Archon's name is Archippos, but since the archonship was held by men of
that name in both 321/0 and 318/7 BC it is uncertain to which year this document
belongs.

ἐπὶ Ἀρχίππου ἄρχοντος Φρυνίωνος δημαρχοῦ[ντος] ‖ [κ]ατὰ τάδε
μισθοῦσιν Πειραιεῖς Παραλίαν καὶ Ἀλμυρί‖[δ]α καὶ τὸ Θησεῖον καὶ τἆλλα
τεμένη ἅπαντα· τοὺς μισ⟨θω⟩‖[σ]αμένους ὑπὲρ· δ': δραχμὰς καθιστάναι
ἀποτίμημα τῆς μ‖[ι]σθώσεως ἀξιόχρεων, τοὺς δὲ ἐντὸς δ' δραχμ⟨ῶ⟩ν
ἐγγυητὴ‖[ν] ἀποδιδόμενον τὰ ἑαυτοῦ τῆς μισθώσεως. ἐπὶ τοῖσδε μ‖[ι]σθοῦσιν
ἀνεπιτίμητα καὶ ατελῆ. ἐὰν δέ τις εἰσφορὰ γ‖[ί]γνηται ἀπὸ τῶν χωρίων τοῦ
τιμήματος, τοὺς δημότας ε‖[ἰ]σφέρειν. τὴν δὲ ὕλιν καὶ τὴν γῆν μὴ ἐξέστω
ἐξάγειν το‖[ὺ]ς μισθωσαμένους, μήτε ἐκ τοῦ Θησείου μήτε ἐκ τῶν ἄλλ|ων
τεμενῶν, μηδὲ τὴν ὕλην ⟨ἄ⟩λλ°οσ᾽ ἢ τῶι χωρίωι. οἱ μισ⟨θω⟩‖σάμενοι τὸ
Θεσμοφόριον καὶ τὸ τοῦ Σχοινοῦντος καὶ ⟨ὅ⟩σ'‖ ἄλλα ἐννόμια τὴν
μίσθω⟨σ⟩ιν καταθήσουσι τὴμ μὲν ἡμι|έαν ἐν τῶι Ἑκατομβαιῶνι, τὴν δὲ
ἡμισέαν ἐν τῶι Ποσιδε‖ῶνι. οἱ μισθωσάμενοι Παραλίαν καὶ Ἀλμυρίδα καὶ

24 Regulations for the lease of public land by the deme Piraeus, 321/0 BC.
BM GR 1785.5–27.9.

τὸ Θη|σεῖον καὶ τἄλλα εἴ πού τι ἐστίν, ὅσα οἷόν τε καὶ θεμιτόν | ἐστιν
ἐργάσιμα ποεῖν, κατὰ τάδε ἐργάσονται, τὰ μὲν ἐ|ννέα ἔτη ὅπως ἂν
βούλωνται, τῶι δὲ δεκάτωι ἔτ⟨ε⟩ι τὴν ἡ|μισέαν ἀροῦν καὶ μὴ πλεί⟨ω⟩, ὅπως
ἂν τῶι μισθωσαμένωι | μετὰ ταῦτα ἐξῆι ὑπεργάζεσθαι ἀπὸ τῆς ἕκτης ἐπὶ
δέκ|α τοῦ Ἀνθεστηριῶνος· ἐὰν δὲ πλείω ἀρόσηι ἢ τὴν ἡμισέ|αν, τῶν
δημοτῶν ἔστω ὁ καρπὸς ὁ πλείων. τὴν οἰκίαν τὴ[ν] | ἐν Ἁλμυπ|ίδι
στέγουσαν παραλαβὼν καὶ ὀρθὴν κατὰ τ[..] | [− − − − − − −ᶜᵃ· ³⁰− − − − − − −]
τ. ονορθαὶ[...]

In the time of Archippos as Archon, Phrynion as Demarch. In accordance with the
following terms the people of Piraeus lease Paralia and Halmyris and the Theseion
and all the other precincts; those leasing for more than 10 drachmas are to
provide a security of a value equivalent to the rent; for those leasing for less than
10 drachmas, the guarantor is to give his own property as security for the loan.
Under these conditions they lease without rates and without taxes; but if any War
Tax is levied on the valuation of the property, the demesmen are to contribute.
And the Lessors shall not be permitted to remove the mud (?wood) or the soil,
neither from the Theseion nor from the other precincts, nor (to carry off) the
wood elsewhere than to the property. Those leasing the Thesmophorion and the
(place) of the reed-growing and any other (places) covered by legislation shall pay
the rent half in the (month of) Hekatombaion and half in the (month of)
Poseideion. Those leasing Paralia and Halmyris and the Theseion and the other
places if there are any, so far as it is possible and proper to bring (them) into
cultivation, shall cultivate them as follows: for nine years however they wish, but in

the tenth year (they are) to till for half the year and no more, so that it shall be possible for the one who leases subsequently to plough up from the 16th of (the month of the) Anthesteria. And if he tills for more than the half year, the excess crop shall belong to the deme[smen]. Taking over the roofed house in Halmyris … (he shall maintain it?) upright …

It is possible that ὕλιν ('mud') in the ninth line was an error by the stonecutter for ὕλην ('wood'). The stonecutter certainly made several other errors, including *alpha* and *lamda* for *omega* in the fifth and nineteenth lines, *lamda* for *alpha* in the eleventh, *eta* for *epsilon* in the eighteenth, *omicron* omitted near the end of the twelfth, and blank spaces for *sigma* in the middle of the thirteenth and for *theta omega* at the end of the eleventh.

The next group of inscriptions from Athens date from before 403/2 BC and make use of the Attic alphabet. The chief difference among the consonants is that ∧ represents *gamma*, not (as in the Ionic alphabet) *lamda*, which in Attic is written ∟. The sign H (*heta*) is still used as the aspirate (and is transliterated as *h*) rather than as the 'long' form of the vowel 'e'. In the Attic alphabet both 'long' and 'short' forms as well as the diphthong 'ei' are represented by *epsilon*, and *omicron* stands not only for the 'long' and 'short' forms of 'o' but also for most cases of the diphthong 'ou'. Since the double consonants *xi* and *psi* have not yet been introduced, the sounds they represent are written as *chi sigma* (Χ𐤎) and *phi sigma* (Φ𐤎). *Sigma* itself was often written with four bars (𐌔) in the Ionic fashion before the use of the Ionic alphabet became mandatory. A few scattered examples occur even before 500 BC, and after about the middle of the fifth century the old three-barred sigma (𐤎) gradually dropped out of use.

The attractive appearance of so many of the official inscriptions of the Athenian democracy in the later fifth century BC is largely achieved by a combination of a classically simple style of lettering with a strict adherence to the discipline of the *stoichedon* arrangement. Although the work of particular stonecutters can sometimes be recognised in groups of inscriptions, in the absence of signatures or other records not one of these men is known to us by name.

It was the Athenian custom in time of war to commemorate each year the men who fell on active service. The famous funeral oration, which Thucydides puts into the mouth of Perikles at the end of the first year of the Peloponnesian War, is a model of a speech for such an occasion. A memorial was also provided at public expense. In 432 BC, shortly before the Peloponnesian War itself broke out, the Athenians saw action at Potidaea. Thucydides tells us that the Athenian victory came quickly, whereupon some of the Potidaeans fled to the walls. 'After the battle', he goes on, 'the Athenians set up a trophy and they surrendered the dead under truce to the Potidaeans. Of the Potidaeans and their allies not far short of 300 were killed, of the Athenians themselves 150 men and Kallias the General.' A single slab survives from the monument built in Athens to commemorate Kallias and his men. The inscription includes twelve lines of verse that evidently comprised three epigrams of four lines each. The first is very fragmentary, but the other two may be restored with some confidence. In one the flight of some of the Potidaeans, which was described by Thucydides, is contrasted with the honourable fate of the dead. A small fragment of the same inscription, which was found in the Athenian agora in 1935, preserves a few letters from the ends of the last three lines, so confirming the restorations proposed in earlier publications.

25

αἰθὲρ μὲμ φσυχὰς ὑπεδέχσατο σόμ[ατα δὲ χθὸν]
τὸνδε Ποτειδαίας δ᾿ ἀμφὶ πύλας ἐλ[ύθεν].
ἐχθρὸν δ᾿ οἱ μὲν ἔχοσι τάφο μέρος, h[οι δὲ φυγόντες]

τεῖχος πιστοτάτεν hελπίδ' ἔθεντο [βίου].
ἄνδρας μὲμ πόλις hέδε ποθεῖ καὶ δ<u>ε</u>[μος Ἐρεχθέος]
   πρόσθε Ποτειδαίας hοὶ θα[νον ἐμ προ[ο]μάχοις,
παῖδες Ἀθεναίον, φσυχὰς δ' ἀντίρρο[π]α θέντες
   ἐ[λλ]άχσαντ' ἀρετὲν καὶ πατρ[ίδ'] εὐκλ[έ]ϊσαν.

The air received the spirits and [the earth] the bodies of these men, and [they were undone] around the gates of Potidaea; of their enemies some attained the destiny of the grave, others [fled and] made the wall their surest hope [of life].

This city and the people [of Erechtheus] mourn the men who died in [battle] before Potidaea, sons of Athenians; [placing] their lives as a counterpoise they received glory in exchange and brought honour to their native land.

25   Epitaph for the Athenian casualties at Potidaea, 432 BC. BM GR 1816.6–10.348.

The inscription for the men who fell at Potidaea in 432 doubtless included a list of their names, which has not survived. Among related inscriptions that have survived is a list of Athenians who were killed on active service in a single year during the Peloponnesian War. Some parts of the list are difficult to read since the surface of the stone has been damaged and a number of letters are illegible. A fairly easy section appears about half-way down the first column.

Ἀντιοχίδος	of (the tribe) Antiochis
Ἀριστομέδες	Aristomedes
Ἀμεινοκλῆς	Ameinokles
Αἰσχίνες	Aischines
Παντακλῆς	Pantakles
Χαρίδεμος	Charidemos
Τιμόχσενος	Timoxenos
Ἀντιφάνης	Antiphanes
ἐμ Ποτειδαίαι	in Potidaea
Παντακλῆς	Pantakles
Ἁγνόδεμος	Hagnodemos
Ἀρχίας	Archias
ἐν Ἀμφιπόλει	in Amphipolis
Φιλόφρον	Philophron

The men's names are grouped according to their tribes, and the first word in each section is the name of the tribe. There is a blank line at the end of each section before the next heading. The name of Antiphanes was added later in this space: the letters do

26 List of Athenian casualties, 425/4 or 424/3 BC. BM GR 1816.6-10.173.

not conform to the *stoichedon* pattern, and the stonecutter has used H for *eta*. Since the names of the tribes recur in each column, it seems likely that the casualties of two major engagements head the list, but the exact locations are not known since the upper part of the slab is missing. At the foot of the first column are the names of those who fell at Potidaea and Amphipolis, in Thrace and at Pylos, Sermylia and Singos. It has been suggested that most of these campaigns can be placed in 424 BC, and that the casualty from Pylos died of wounds received there in the previous year. Non-citizens who gave their lives are listed at the end of the second column under three headings: *engraphoi* ('enrolled men'), *toxotai* ('archers') and *xenoi* ('aliens').

To the historian the records of the valuable gifts presented from time to time to the 27
goddess Athena provide an insight into the working of the Athenian democracy. Commissions of citizens, including a chairman and a secretary, were appointed annually to be responsible for the treasures. An inventory was taken each year when responsibility was handed over from one commission to the next, and the lists seem to have been recorded permanently on stone every four years on the occasion of the Great Panathenaia. To the epigrapher the repetitive nature of the lists provides an opportunity to restore with almost complete certainty the gaps in the text caused by damage to the surviving slabs. The texts themselves provide many examples of the acrophonic system of numerals. One drachma is represented by ⊢ and one obol by I. The account of the treasures kept in the *pronaos* ('front porch') of the Parthenon for the year 414/3 BC, for the first year of a four-yearly cycle, begins as follows:

> *[τάδ]ε [παρέδο]σαν hαι τέτταρες ἀρχ[αί, hαὶ ἐδίδοσαν τὸν λόγον ἐκ Παναθε̄ναίο̄ν ἐς Παναθε̄́ναια* vvv*] | [τοῖ]ς ταμίαις Τεισαμενο̄͂ι Παιαν[ιεῖ καὶ χσυνάρχοσι hοῖς Πολυμε̄́δε̄ς Κε̄φισιο̄́νος Ἀτε̄νεὺς ἐγρα]||[μμά]τευε· hοι δὲ ταμίαι, hοῖς Πολυ[με̄́δε̄ς Κε̄φισιο̄́νος Ἀτε̄νεὺς ἐγραμμάτευε, παρέδοσαν τοῖς ταμ* v*]||[ίαις] Πολυχσενίδε̄ι Ἀχαρνεῖ καὶ χ[συνάρχοσι, hοῖς Λευκαῖος*

27   Inventory of treasurers in the Parthenon, 414/13 and 413/12 BC. BM GR 1816.6–10.282.

Κōμάρχο Ἀφιδναῖος ἐγραμμάτευε, ᵛ‖ *[ἐν τōι] πρόνεōι· φιάλε͂ χρυσε͂ ἐχς ε͂ς*
ἀ|ποραίνονται, ἄσταθμος· φιάλαι ἀργυραῖ ΗΔΔⵏ, *σταθμὸν τού*ᵛᵛ‖*[τōν*
ΤΤ|ΗΗΗΗΔΔⵏⵏ· *κέρατα ἀργυρᾶ* ⅢⅠ, *[σταθμὸν τούτōν* ⵏ□ΔΔⵏⵏⵏ·
ποτέ́ρια ἀργυρᾶ ⵏ, *σταθμὸν τούτōν* ᵛ]‖[Η□Δⵏⵏⵏ·] *λύχνος ἀργυρὸς,*
σταθμὸν τ[ούτο ΔΔΔⵏⵏⵏ·

These (are the) things (that) the four commissions who rendered the account from
Panathenaia to Panathenaia handed over to the stewards Teisamenos of Paiania
and his colleagues for whom Polymedes (son) of Kephision of Atene was secretary;
and (the things that) the stewards for whom Polymedes (son) of Kephision was
secretary handed over to the stewards Polyxenides of Acharnai and his colleagues,
for whom Leukaios (son) of Komarchos of Aphidnai was secretary, in the *pronaos*:
a golden libation bowl, from which they sprinkle themselves, unweighed; 121
silver libation bowls, the weight of these 2 Talents 432 Drachmas; 3 silver drinking
horns, the weight of these 528 Drachmas; 5 silver cups, the weight of these 167
Drachmas; a silver lamp, the weight of this 38 Drachmas…

In the three remaining years of the cycle the preamble is different. The account for
413/2 BC begins:

[τάδε hoι] ταμίαι τὸν hιερōν χρέμ[άτōν] τε͂ς Ἀθεναίας Πο[λυχσενίδες
Ἀχαρνεὺς καὶ χσυνάρχοντες,]|[hοῖς Λευ]καῖος Κōμάρχο Ἀφιδνα[ῖος
ἐ]γραμμάτευε, παρ[έδοσαν τοῖς ταμίαις, hοῖς Αὐτοκλείδες ᵛᵛ]‖[Σōστράτ]ο
Φρεάρριος ἐγραμμάτ[ευε, Κ]αλλαίσχρōι Εὐπ[υρίδει καὶ χσυνάρχοσι
παραδεχσάμενοι ᵛ]|[παρὰ τὸν] προτέρōν ταμιōν, hοῖς [Πολυ]μέδες*
Κεφισιόν[ος Ἀτενεὺς ἐγραμμάτευε, ἐν τōι πρόνεōι· ᵛᵛ]

These (are the) things the stewards of the sacred monies of Athena, Polyxenides of
Acharnai and his colleagues, for whom Leukaios (son) of Komarchos of Aphidnai
was secretary, handed over to the stewards for whom Autokleides (son) of
Sostratos of Phrearoi was secretary, Kallaischros of Eupyridai and his colleagues
having received (them) from the previous stewards, for whom Polymedes (son) of
Kephision of Atene was secretary, in the *pronaos* …

It is not known for certain when construction began on the temple on the Athenian
acropolis now known as the Erechtheion. It was probably some time after 421 BC, but
work was later postponed at a date that is also not recorded. In the late summer of
409 BC the Athenian Assembly passed a decree proposed by Epigenes appointing a

28   Report of the Building Commission for the Erechtheion at Athens, 409/8 BC.
BM GR 1785.5–27.1.

Commission to complete the temple. The date is given in the prescript of a long   28
inscription, in which the Commission recorded its progress during the first year: the
decree was passed during the first session of the Council in the archonship of Diokles,
who took office in 409 BC. The three commissioners included Chariades from Agryle,
who was one of the Treasurers of the Delian League (Hellenotamias) in 408/7 BC, and
was evidently a man of some standing. Assisted by an architect and a secretary, the
Commissioners began by carrying out a detailed survey of the building so far as it had
been completed and by compiling an inventory of the blocks, both finished and un-
finished, that were lying around the site. Their first report also includes details of
blocks set in place that year.

[ἐ]πιστάται τô νεô τô ἐμ πόλει ἐν hôι τὸ ἀρχαῖον ἄγαλμα, Βροσυν[ί]-
[δ]ὲς Κέφισιεύς, Χαριάδες Ἀγρυλêθεν, Διόδες Κέφισιεύς, ἀρχιτέκτο[ν]
[Φι]λοκλês Ἀχαρνεύς, γραμματεὺς Ἐτέαρχος Κυδαθêναιεύς,
[τά]δε ἀνέγραφσαν ἔργα τô νεô hôς κατέλαβον ἔχοντα κατὰ τὸ φσέ-
[φι]σμα τô δέμο hὸ Ἐπιγένες εἶπεν ἐχσεργασμένα καὶ hêμίεργα ἐπὶ Διο-
[κ]λέος ἄρχοντος, Κεκροπίδος πρυτανευόσες πρότες ἐπὶ τês βολês
[h]êι Νικοφάνες Μαραθόνιος πρôτος ἐγραμμάτευσεν.

τô νεô τάδε κατελάβομεν hεμίεργα·
ἐπὶ τêι γονίαι τêι πρὸς τô Κεκροπίο·
    πλίνθος ἀθέτος μêκος τετρά-
IIII ποδας, πλάτος δίποδας, πάχος
    τριhεμιποδίος.
    μασχαλιαίαν μêκος τετράποδα,
I   πλάτος τρίποδα, πάχος τριôν
    hεμιποδίôν.
    ἐπικρανίτιδας μêκος τετράπο-

Γ   δας, πλάτος τρίποδας, πάχος
τριῶν ἡεμιποδίōν.
γονιαίαν μêκος ἡεπτάποδα,

[Ι]   πλάτος τετράποδα, πάχος
τριῶν ἡεμιποδίōν.
γογγύλος λίθος ἄθετος, ἀντίμο-

[Ι]   ρος ταῖς ἐπικρανίτισιν μêκος
δεκάπος, ἡύφσος τριōν
ἡεμιποδίōν.

The Commissioners of the temple on the Acropolis, in which (there is) the ancient image: Brosyn...es [Brysonides?] of Kephisia, Chariades from Agryle, Diodes [Dioudes?] of Kephisia, architect [Phi]lokles of Acharnai, secretary Etearchos of Kydathenaion, recorded as follows the work on the temple in the state in which they found it completed or half-finished, in accordance with the decree of the People, in the archonship of Dio[k]les, while the tribe of Kekropis held the first prytany, during (the session of) the Council in which Nikophanes of Marathon was the first to serve as secretary.

We found the following parts of the temple half-finished: at the corner towards the Kekropion:
4 wall-blocks unplaced, length four feet, width two feet, thickness one foot and a half;
1 *maschaliaia*, length four feet, width three feet, thickness one foot and a half;
5 blocks of wall-crown, length four feet, width three feet, thickness one foot and a half;
1 angle-block, length seven feet, width four feet, thickness one foot and a half;
1 moulded block unplaced, backing for the wall-crown, length ten feet, height one foot and a half.

The term *maschaliaia* has not been convincingly explained.

Fragments are preserved in the Epigraphic Museum in Athens of the lower part of this stele and also of related inscriptions that give details of expenditure on the Erechtheion in subsequent years. The account for 408/7 BC names a different architect (Archilochos) from Agryle. Neither he nor Philokles actually designed the building, but they were responsible for supervising the construction.

An earlier inscription with the Attic three-barred *sigma* is carved on three sides of a slab presented to the British Museum in 1781 by the Society of Dilettanti, having been found in a house in Athens by Richard Chandler. The slab is incomplete, and the inscriptions on the principal faces are very fragmentary. They appear to deal with the regulations for various festivals celebrated by the deme Skambonidai. On one occasion the skin of the sacrificial victim is to be the perquisite of the Demarch, perhaps because he had to provide the beast in the first place. The flesh is to be distributed to the people raw.

On the narrow end of the slab is an extract from the deme's financial regulations. The text is well preserved as far as it goes. It includes the end of the oath to be taken on assuming office and the beginning of the regulations for the financial examination normal at the end of a term in public office in Athens.

[.] κ̄ερυχ[θ]‖̂ει:ἐπαγγ|ελθ̂ει:κα|ι̇ τὰ κοιν‖[ὰ] τὰ Σκαμ|βōνιδōν | σōō:καὶ
ἀ|ποδόσō:π|αρὰ τὸν ε‖ῦ̈θυνον:τ|ὸ καθ̂εκο|ν:ταῦτα ἐ|πομνύν̣α|ι̣:τὸς τρ̂ε‖ς
θεός:ἡό|τι ἄν τō[ν] | κοινόν:μ|ὲ̇ ἀποδιδ|ōσιν:παρ‖ὰ τὸν εῦ̈θ|υνο[ν π]ρό| _ _ _

31

29 Epitaph of Chairedemos, *c.* 550 BC. MMA 16.174.6.

… as it may] be heralded (and) announced. I shall both safeguard the common
(property) of the Skambonidai, and I shall return to the Public Examiner what is
due. These things (they are) to swear (by) the three gods. Whatever of the common
(property) they do not give back to the Public Examiner …

The inscription from Skambonidai already has an *epsilon* with vertical and horizontal
strokes and a *theta* in the form of a dot in a circle. At an earlier stage of the development of the Athenian alphabet *epsilon* was written with oblique strokes and the
upright had an extension below the lowest bar; *theta* had a cross rather than a dot in
the circle; and *chi* was sometimes written + rather than X. The two following inscriptions are both written *boustrophedon*. A metrical epitaph on the base of a stele in 29
New York consists of an elegiac couplet (a dactylic hexameter followed by a penta-
meter). The layout of the inscription ignores the verse form, but punctuation is used
to separate some of the words. At the end is an additional comment in prose about
the sculptor, perhaps an actual signature:

Χαιρεδέμο ⋮ τόδε σε̃μα ⋮ πατὲρ ἔστε̃[σε | θ]ανόντος ⋮
Ἀνφιχάρ⟨ε̃⟩ς ⋮ ἀγαθὸν παῖδα ὀ|λοφυρόμενο[ς]
   Φαίδιμος ἐποίε

On the death of Chairedemos his father Amphichares set up this monument
mourning a good son. Phaidimos made it.

In the name of Chairedemos the third syllable should be 'long', but it has been treated
as 'short' in order to force the name into the metre.
   A second Athenian gravestone in New York has a simpler epitaph: Ἀντιγένει ⋮ 30
Παναίσχες ἐπ|έθε̃κεν ('To Antigenes Panaisches set up (this monument)).

30 Epitaph of Antigenes, *c.* 510–500 BC. MMA 15.167.

Another early inscription, also written *boustrophedon*, records the presentation of
32   a wine-bowl and strainer for civic use in the town hall (*prytaneion*) at Sigeion in north-
western Asia Minor. The text is given twice, first in the Ionic dialect and alphabet,
then in Attic with smaller letters and a more detailed text:

Φανοδίκο| ἐμὶ τὸ͜ρμοκ|ρ̄άτεος τō | Π̄ροκοννη|σ̄ίο κρητῆρ|ᾱ δὲ : καὶ
ὑποκ|ρ̄ητήριον : κ|αὶ ἠθμὸν : ἐς π|ρ̄υτανήιον | ἔδωκεν : Συκε|ε͡ῦσιν.

Φανοδίκο : εἰμὶ : τō h|ε͡ρμοκράτος : τō Προκο|ν͡ε͡σίο : κἀγὸ : κρατέρα |
κἀπίστατον : καὶ hε͡θμ|ὸ͡ν : ἐς πρυτανεῖον : ἔ͡δōκα : μνῆμα : Σιγε⟨ι⟩|ε͡ῦσι :
ἐὰν δέ τι πάσχ|ō̄ μελεδαίνεν : με ō̃ | Σ̄ῑγειὲς : καί μ᾽ἐπο|⟨ῑ͡ε̄⟩σεν : haíσōπος :
καὶ | : h͡άδελφοί.

I am (the stele) of Phanodikos (son) of Hermokrates of Prokonnesos; and he gave a
wine-bowl and a stand and a strainer to the Sigeans for the town hall.

I am (the stele) of Phanodikos (son) of Hermokrates of Prokonnesos; and I gave
a wine-bowl and a stand and a strainer to the Sigeans for the town hall as a
memorial; and if I suffer anything, care for me, O Sigeans; and Haisopos and his
brothers made me.

Since Ionic was the dialect of the Sigeans themselves, repetition of the text in Attic
suggests that the stele was set up after the Athenian conquest of the area, which
according to Herodotus took place while Pisistratus was tyrant of Athens. The
precise date of the stele has been the subject of much scholarly controversy, but a
date just after the middle of the sixth century seems to fit both the historical circum-
stances and the style of the inscription.

Another Ionic inscription was brought to London from Ephesos by J. T. Wood, the
33   discoverer of the temple of Artemis. It was part of a long text originally carved on a
wall in columns, twenty-one letters wide, which were separated by vertical lines. In
the adjacent column too few letters survive to permit restoration of the text. The
surviving portion deals with the interpretation of lucky and unlucky signs in the flight
of birds:

[ἐκ μὲν τῆς δεξιῆ]ς εἰς τὴν ἀριστερὴν πετ|όμεν]ος : ἤμ μὲν : ἀποκρύψε|[ι
δε]ξιός, : ἢν δὲ : ἐπάρει : τὴ|[ν ε]ὐώνυμον : πτέρυγα : κἂν ‖ [ἐπά]ρει : κἂν
ἀποκρύ[ψ]ει : ε|[ὐών]υμος, : ἐγ δὲ : τῆς ἀριστ‖[ερῆς] : ἐς τὴν δεξιὴν :
πετό|[με]νος : ἤμ μὲν : ἰθὺς : ἀποκρ|[ύ]ψει : εὐώνυμος, : ἢν δὲ : τὴν ‖
[δεξ]ιὴν : πτέρυγα : ἐπάρας ___

[...flying from right to left], if it goes out of sight, it is lucky; but if it raises its left
wing, whether it rises or goes out of sight, it is unlucky; but flying from the left to
the right, if it goes straight out of sight, it is unlucky, but if raising the right wing...

The beginning of the sentence is missing but the first few words can be restored with
some certainty by comparison with what follows in this rather repetitive text. In
antiquity the left wing was clearly ill-omened.

Although the letter-forms of the Ionic alphabet gradually became standard
throughout Greece from the late fifth century BC, the use of local dialects survived
34   rather longer. An inscription of the later third century from Orchomenos is still in the
Boeotian dialect that was spoken there. It records a contract between the city (called
Erchomenos in Boeotian) and Euboulos (written Eubolos, reflecting Boeotian
pronunciation) of Elateia. Euboulos had lent the city a large sum of money, and the

41

31 *Left* Extract from the financial regulations of the deme Skambonidai at Athens, *c.* 460 BC. BM GR 1785.5–27.2.
32 *Right* Inscription from Sigeion in Ionic and Attic script and dialect, *c.* 550–540 BC. BM GR 1816.6–10.107.

33 *Below* Rules for taking omens from the flight of birds, *c.* 500–475 BC. BM GR 1867.11–22.441.

34 *Left* Loan-agreement between Euboulos of Elateia and the city of Orchomenos, 3rd century BC. BM GR 1816.6–10.377.

35 *Right* Three proxeny-decrees awarding privileges to foreigners at Kalymna, 4th century BC. BM GR 1856.8–26.6.

first two sections of the inscription record two repayments, the second of which liquidated the entire loan. The third section reads:

ἄρχοντος ἐν Ἐρχομενῦ Θυνάρχω, μει|νὸς Ἀλαλκομενίω, ἐν δὲ Φελατίη
Με|νοίταο Ἀρχελάω, μεινὸς πράτω, ὁμο|λογ(ί)α Εὐβώλυ Φελατιῆϋ κὴ τῆ
πόλι Ἐρ‖χομενίων· ἐπιδεὶ κεκόμιστη Εὔβω|λος πὰρ τὰς πόλιος τὸ δάνειον
ἄπαν | καττὰς ὁμολογίας τὰς τεθεῖσας Θυ|νάρχω ἄρχοντος, μεινὸς
Θειλουθίω, | κὴ οὔτ᾽ ὀφείλετη αὐτῦ ἔτι οὐθὲν πὰρ τὰν ‖ πόλιν ἀλλ᾽ ἀπέχι
πάντα περὶ παντὸς | κὴ ἀποδεδόανθι τῆ πόλι τὺ ἔχοντες | τὰς ὁμολογίας,
εἶμεν ποτιδεδομέ|νον χρόνον Εὐβώλυ ἐπινομίας Φέτια | πέτταρα βόυεσσι
σοὺν ἵππυς διακα‖τίης Φίκατι προβάτυς σοὺν ἤγυς χει|λίης· ἄρχι τῶ χρόνω
ὁ ἐνιαυτὸς ὁ μετὰ | Θύναρχον ἄρχοντα Ἐρχομενίυς· ἀπ[ο]‖γράφεσθη δὲ
Εὔβωλον κατ᾽ ἐνιαυτὸν | ἔκαστον πὰρ τὸν ταμίαν κὴ τὸν νομώ‖ναν τά τε
καύματα τῶν προβάτων κὴ | τᾶν ἤγων κὴ τᾶν βουῶν κὴ τᾶν ἵππων κ[ὴ] | κά
τινα ἄσαμα ἴωνθι κὴ τὸ πλεῖθος, με[ὶ] | ἀπογραφέσθω δὲ πλίονα τῶν
γεγραμ|μένων ἐν τῆ σουγχωρείσι. ἠ δέ κά τις ‖ |πράτ|τη τὸ ἐννόμιον
Εὔβωλον, ὀφειλέ‖|τω ἀ πόλις τῶν Ἐρχομενίων ἀργουρίω | |μνᾶς|
πετταράκοντα Εὐβώλυ καθ᾽ ἔκα‖|στον ἐ|νιαυτὸν, κ[ὴ] τόκον φερέτω δρά Ⅲ| |
[κατὰ] τὰς μνᾶς ἐκάστας κατὰ μεῖνα ‖|ἔκασ|τον κὴ ἔμπρακτος ἔστω
Εὐβ[ώλυ | ἀ πόλις] τῶν Ἐρχ[ο]|μεν[ίων]

During the archonship of Thunarchos in Orchomenos, month of Alalkomenios, and of Menoitas (son) of Archelaos in Elateia, first month; an agreement between Euboulos of Elateia and the city of Orchomenos: whereas Euboulos has recovered from the city the whole loan according to the agreements made during the archonship of Thunarchos, month of Theilouthios, and nothing is still owed to him by the city, but he has received everything in full, and those having the contracts have restored (them) to the city, there shall be an additional period for Euboulos of right of free pasturage for four years for 220 oxen and horses and 1,000 sheep and goats; the year after the archonship of Thunarchos at Orchomenos begins the period; and Euboulos shall register every year with the Treasurer and the Land Agent the brands of the sheep and the goats and the oxen and the horses, and any that go without a brand, and the total; and he shall not register more than written in the agreement. And if anyone imposes dues for pasture on Euboulos, the city of Orchomenos shall owe Euboulos 40 minas of silver each year, and it shall bear interest of 3 drachmas for each mina every month, and the city of Orchomenos shall be under bond to Euboulos…

Since there is no mention of interest on the loan, it seems likely that in lieu of interest Euboulos was allowed to graze his animals on the common land of Orchomenos without charge. The size of the payments suggests that the loan was repaid earlier than had originally been stipulated. Euboulos, having expected to have a longer period of free pasturage under the original contract, is thus compensated by a grant of free pasturage for four years, beginning at the end of the year in which repayments were made (the archonship of Thunarchos). Provision is made to indemnify Euboulos if anyone imposes charges for pasturage, to which under the contract he is entitled free of charge.

The use of the Doric dialect also survives in inscriptions from the island of Kalymna. A single stele found at the temple of Apollo records three decrees conferring the title of Proxenos and various privileges on foreigners. A *proxenos* performed some of the functions of a modern Vice-Consul, helping foreign citizens, for example, by representing them in the law courts, to which as foreigners they had no right of access. Such services could be provided for each other by private citizens of different cities, but if a man regularly assisted visitors (usually merchants) from a particular city, it was customary to recognise this officially. The first two decrees also confer the title of Euergetes ('Benefactor') and are dated by the month and the year (the year specified as usual by the name of the chief magistrate):

ἔδοξε τᾶι ἐκκλησίαι τᾶι Καλυ|μνίων, μηνὸς Ἀρταμιτίου ἐπ᾽ Ἀ|ριστολαΐδα,
Παρμενίσκον τὸν Ἀλεξιδίκου ἦμεν εὐεργέταν κα[ὶ] ‖ πρόξενον Καλυμνίων
καὶ αὐτὸ[ν] | καὶ γένος ἀεὶ καὶ ἦμεν αὐτοῖς ἔγ|κτησιν ἐγ Καλύμναι καὶ
ἀτέλεια[ν] | τῶν ἐξαγομένων καὶ ἐσαγομένων | καὶ ἐμ πολέμωι καὶ ἐν
ἰράναι. ‖

   Θεός

ἔδοξε τᾶι ἐκκλησίαι τᾶι Καλυμνί|ων, μηνὸς Καρνείου, ἐπὶ Λευκάρου, |
Διοσκουρίδαν τὸν Δελφὸν καὶ Ἀλε|ξίδικον εὐεργέτας καὶ προξένους ‖ ἦμεν
Καλυμνίων καὶ αὐτοὺς καὶ ἐκγό|νους καὶ ἦμεν αὐτοῖς ἐγ Καλύμναι |
ἀτέλειαν τῶν ἐσαγομένων καὶ ἐξα|γομένων καὶ ἔσπλον καὶ ἔκπλον καὶ |
ἐμ πολέμωι καὶ ἐν ἰράναι.

Decreed by the Assembly of Kalymna, in the month of Artemitios, under Aristolaidas: Parmeniskos son of Alexidikos to be a benefactor and a *proxenos* of Kalymna, both himself and his family in perpetuity, and to have the right to own property in Kalymna and immunity from taxation on exports and imports both in war and in peace.

   God (grant good fortune)

Decreed by the Assembly of Kalymna, in the month of Karneios, under Leukaros: Dioskourides of Delphi and Alexidikos to be benefactors and *proxenoi* of Kalymna, both themselves and their descendants, and to have in Kalymna immunity from taxation on imports and exports and the right to sail in and out in war and in peace.

The decrees vary slightly in particulars and even in vocabulary, presumably because they were framed in the meeting of the assembly rather than drafted in detail first. Thus, although all three make the titles hereditary, no particular significance should be attached to the use of the word for 'family' (*genos*) rather than 'descendants' (*ekogonoi*) in the decree for Parmeniskos, no for the omission in his case of the right of sailing in and out, which may be taken as implied by the tax-exemption on imports and exports. The right to own real property (*egktesis*), however, was a very valuable privilege rarely conferred on foreigners.

The most famous Greek inscription in the British Museum is probably the Rosetta Stone, which derives its importance not from the intrinsic interest of the text but from the presence on the same slab of translations into ancient Egyptian in both the hieroglyphic and demotic scripts. Study of the Rosetta Stone was crucial for the decipherment of Egyptian writing. The text records a long and rather sycophantic decree passed by the general council of Egyptian priests, in which honours are bestowed on Ptolemy V Epiphanes in recognition of his services to Egypt both at home and abroad. The Greek text abounds in errors. The first line begins: βασιλεύοντος τοῦ νέου καὶ παραλ⟨α⟩βόντος τὴν β⟨α⟩σιλείαν παρὰ τοῦ πατρὸς ('In the reign of the young one, who has taken over the kingdom from his father…'). The stonecutter has twice written Λ (*lamda*) for Α (*alpha*), the correct readings being given in angled brackets in the transcription. Other errors elsewhere in the text include Ξ (*xi*) for Σ

36

36   Part of the Rosetta Stone, 27 March 196 BC. BM EA 24.

(*sigma*), H (*eta*) for II (*iota* twice, at the end of one word and the beginning of the next) and II for H (that is, *eta* with the bar missing), as well as letters left out altogether: Πτομαίου for Πτο⟨λε⟩μαίου. The text concludes with a provision that has many parallels in earlier Greek inscriptions: '[This decree shall be inscribed on a slab] of hard stone in hieroglyphic, demotic and Greek characters and set up in each of the first, second [and third (rank) temples beside the image of the ever-living King].' The restorations are based on the demotic text.

3
Inscriptions on Other Objects

Apart from epitaphs and votives most inscriptions on stone slabs are public rather than private in character. Inscriptions on other objects, however, are usually private. Dedications and statements of ownership are particularly frequent on bronzes and pottery. They are regularly added after the manufacture of the object itself, cut or scratched into the surface. Scratched inscriptions on pottery are known as *graffiti*, while inscriptions painted on pottery after manufacture are called *dipinti*. *Dipinti* referring to trade, often painted on the underside of figured vases, are usually faint and difficult to interpret. Other *dipinti* include the epitaphs written in ink with a reed pen on cinerary urns from Alexandria. Inscriptions applied to vases during manufacture include signatures of potters and painters, the names of the figures and other comments. Pottery and bronze vessels given as prizes in competitions were appropriately inscribed during manufacture. These may be classified as public inscriptions, which were not confined to stone slabs.

As with inscriptions on stone slabs, the simpler inscriptions on other objects can be read with little or no knowledge of Greek beyond the alphabet. For example, the first twenty letters of the alphabet (*alpha* to *upsilon*) are inscribed in sequence on a stone *eikosahedron* (a geometrically regular solid object with twenty triangular faces). It is likely to have been used as a die in a game of chance: the ancients also used six-sided dice marked in the same way as their modern counterparts, but on the *eikosahedron* the absence of *digamma*, the alphabetic numeral for six, shows that the letters are not used here as numerals but have a purely alphabetic value. The relatively late date is shown by the broken crossbar on the *alpha* and the lunate *sigma*.

In order to ensure fair trading many Greek cities maintained official standards of volume and weight, appointing *agoranomoi*, market-clerks or, as we might call them, Inspectors of Weights and Measures, to enforce the regulations. A lead weight of one mina (100 drachmai), issued in the fourth year of an unnamed ruler, bears around its edge the names of Zenobios, who was perhaps the *agoranomos*: ἔτους δ′ | δημόσια | μνᾶ | Ζηνοβίου ('Year 4. Official mina. (Of) Zenobios').

The name of an Athenian citizen with his father's name (patronymic) and their deme (demotic) is clearly inscribed on a small rectangular bronze plate about 11.6 cm long, 2.0 cm wide and 2 mm thick: Ἀριστοφῶν ⫶ Ἀρισ|τοδήμου ⫶ Κοθω(κίδης) ('Aristophon (son) of Aristodemos (of the deme) Kotho(kidai)'). Aristophon and other members of his family are known also from other inscriptions, including grave-stelae. His brother Exekestides was wealthy enough to fit out a trireme in 353/2 BC.

Bronze plates like this were used to identify jurymen, or dikasts, and to assign them to particular cases in the courts. In order to ensure a fair trial and prevent bribery Athenian juries were very large, and the selection of jurymen took place just before cases were heard. Prospective jurymen inserted their tickets according to their allocated section letter (in this case *gamma*) in slots in a marble slab that stood at the entrance to the law courts. The slots were arranged in columns and rows, and at the side was a tube into which black and white balls were poured at random. Men whose tickets were in rows opposite white balls were selected for the jury. The procedure is described by Aristotle (*Constitution of Athens* 63.4), although by his day boxwood had replaced bronze as the material of dikasts' tickets.

Dikasts' tickets were issued by the state and authenticated with official stamps. The owl at the lower left served also as the design of the three-obol coin, an allusion to the juryman's pay of three obols a day, after 424 BC. The *gorgoneion* has been interpreted as signifying that the holder was also eligible to participate in the annual allotment of magistracies.

In order to prevent unauthorised transfer of tickets holes were bored through the plate in patterns appropriate to the letters. When tickets were officially reissued to other citizens, the old holes were allowed to remain and provide clues to the previous name, even when the actual lines of the letters had been obliterated. In this case the previous owner's name has been read as: *Φιλοχάρης | Ἀλαι(εύς)* ('Philochares of Halaï').

The lunate *sigma* (Ϲ), the similar *epsilon* (Ε) and the cursive forms of *mu* (Ϻ) and *omega* (ω) are more suitable than angular letters for writing in ink on papyrus and parchment or on harder surfaces like wood and pottery. From the third century BC onwards the style of handwriting diverged increasingly from that of monumental lettering in stone. The third- and second-century BC cemeteries at Alexandria in Egypt have yielded large numbers of hydriai used as urns for the ashes of the dead. They are known as Hadra vases after an Alexandrian suburb where they were first found in quantity during the nineteenth century. Some of them carry commemorative

37   *Left* Stone eikosahedron with part of the alphabet, Roman period. BM GR 1891.6–24.38.
38   *Right* Lead weight of 1 mina, 2nd or 1st century BC. BM GR 1925.7–20.1.

39   *Below* Bronze juryman's ticket from Athens, mid-4th century . BM GR 1873.8–20.129.

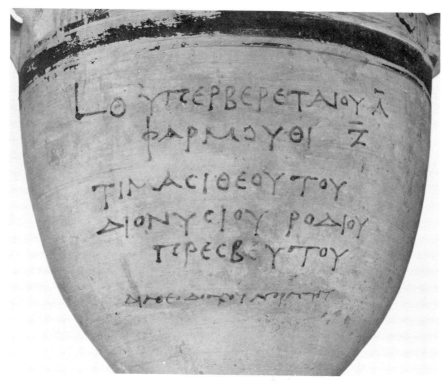

40   Dated Hadra vase, 19 May 213 BC. MMA 90.9.29.

inscriptions, usually written in ink. When the dead man was an official visitor, an ambassador or the like, the inscription may include the signature of the Alexandrian official who arranged the funeral, as well as the date. In addition to the regnal year dates may include the month according to either the Egyptian or the Macedonian calendar. One Hadra vase in New York is dated by both calendars, the Greek month being given first:

˪ θ' Ὑπερβερεταίου λ' | Φαρμουθὶ ζ' | Τιμασιθέου τοῦ | Διονισίου Ῥοδίου ‖ πρεσβευτοῦ | διὰ Θεοδότου ἀγοραστοῦ.

Year 9, Hyperberetaios 30, Pharmouthi 7; Timasitheos (son) of Dionysios of Rhodes, an Ambassador; by Theodotos, agent.

Theodotos, who was active in the reign of Ptolemy IV, signs himself as *agorastes*, which literally means 'buyer': it is here translated as 'agent' by analogy with the Crown Agents, who act as financial agents for nearly 100 governments overseas and for many other official bodies. From other inscriptions, especially on papyri, scholars have been able to prepare a table of the relationship between the Egyptian and the Julian calendars, from which it has been calculated Pharmouthi 7 in the ninth year of Ptolemy IV was the equivalent of 19 May 213 BC.

Also from Egypt comes a wooden board in London with an extract from the first book of Homer's *Iliad* (lines 467–73) written on it in ink. It has an iron handle at the top for carrying or suspension, perhaps in a schoolroom. The wood has cracked along the grain, and the lower part has not survived. The text is written on a thin layer of kaolinite clay, and where this has been abraded the letters have also of course been lost. The losses include the whole of the top line (467) and parts of most others, especially at the right-hand side.

41　Wooden board with a quotation from Homer's *Iliad*, from Egypt, Roman period.
BM GR 1906.10–20.2.

[αὐτὰρ ἐπεὶ παύσαντο πόνου τετύκοντό τε δαῖτα,]
δαίννυθ᾽ / οὐδέ τι / θυμὸ[ς ἐδεύετο δαιτὸς ἐΐσης.]
αὐτὰρ / ἐπεὶ / πόσνος / καὶ / ἐδ[ητύος] ἐξ ἔρον ἔντο,
κοῦροι / μὲν [...] κρητῆρας / ἐπεστέψαντο / ποτοῖο,
νώμησαν δ᾽ / ἄρα / πᾶσιν / ἐπαρξάμενοι / [δ]επάεσσιν·
οἱ δὲ / πανημέριοι / μολπῇ / θεὸ[ν ἱλάσκοντο,]
καλὸν / ἀείδοντες / παιήον[α, κοῦροι Ἀχαιῶν.]

[But when they had ceased from labour and had prepared the banquet,] they
feasted, nor did their appetite [lack anything of the shared feast.] But when of drink
and [food they had satisfied their desire,] youths filled the bowls with wine and
served it to everyone, pouring the first drops in the cups for a libation. So all day
long with song [they appeased the gods,] singing the beautiful paean...

In addition to the usual cursive letters (including ω for *omega*, which does not occur
on the Hadra vase) there is a new way of writing *alpha* (ⱥ), a forerunner of the mini-
scule or lower-case form. The extended right-hand strokes of both *delta* and *lamda*
also anticipate the lower-case forms of these letters. The divisions between words are
marked by oblique strokes, and breathings and accents appear sporadically, not
always in the form that the grammarians would consider 'correct' – for example,
θῦμος not θυμός. In the last line but one παναμέριοι has been corrected to
πανημέριοι. The first surviving word, δαίννυθ᾽, is more usually written δαίννντ᾽: it
is not clear whether the aspirate *theta* represents a local pronunciation where the
non-aspirated *tau* is normal, or is simply another mistake. The same is true of
πόσνος for πόσιος in line 469.

Although individual letter-forms from the Ionic alphabet gradually came into use
in Athens in private inscriptions before their use became obligatory for official
inscriptions in 403/2 BC, texts on Athenian vases and bronzes are mainly in the Attic
alphabet before that date. Many thousands of Athenian vases, both black-figured and
red-figured, have been attributed to individual artists whose particular style of draw-
ing can be recognised and distinguished from others. Since none of these potters and
painters are mentioned in ancient literature, most are unknown to us by name and
have been given nicknames like the Painter of London B 46. Their real names are
known to us only if they actually signed their work, as did Tleson: *Τλέσον ho*
Νεάρχο ἐποίεσεν ('Tleson the (son) of Nearchos made (me)'). Tleson is rare among
potters in including his patronymic, perhaps because his father, Nearchos, was also a

43 distinguished potter who used to sign his works. Most potters and vase-painters signed with their own name only: Ἐχσεκίας ἐποίεσε ('Exekias made (me)'). The signature is written retrograde (right to left).

Exekias has decorated his amphora with a picture of a Greek slaying an Amazon, and has thoughtfully included their names – Achilles (Ἀχιλεύ[ς]) and Penthesilea (Πενθεσιλέα). He has also added a comment on one of the elegant youths of his day: 'Onetorides (is) fair' (Ὀνἒτορίδες καλός). Such comments are fairly common on Attic vases, and since some of the youths referred to later became distinguished in public life, their names can provide useful clues to the dates of the vases that mention them.

44 Although Exekias signed the amphora with Achilles and Penthesilea only as potter, the painting too can be attributed to his hand since he also signed two other vases as painter, and the style is evidently the same. Among other Athenian vase-painters who signed their works the earliest to do so was Sophilos, who decorated an elaborate wine-bowl with a scene of guests arriving for the wedding of Peleus and Thetis. Peleus (Π̅ε̅λεύς) is standing at the door of his house to welcome the guests as they arrive. Iris (Ῑ̅ρις), the messenger, leads the procession, followed by Hestia (ηεστία) and Demeter (Δἒμἒτἒ[ρ]). The names of Peleus and Iris are written retrograde, as is the signature on the wall of the house: Σόφιλος ⋮ μ' ἔγραφσεν ('Sophilos painted me'). Since the composite letter *psi* did not exist in the Attic alphabet, Sophilos wrote the sound as *phi sigma* (ΦΣ). He also used the early closed form of the aspirate (Β), whereas a generation or so later Tleson used the open form (Η).

1 Names can also be added to scenes from daily life to give them a personal quality. The vase-painter Oltos identified all the figures in a scene in the *palaestra* ('gymnasium') on a *psykter* ('wine-cooler') now in New York. On the left in fig. 1 is a javelin-thrower named Batrachos (Β Ρ · · Α Τ Ο Σ Βά[τρ]αχος). The jumper's name is Dorotheos (ϱ Ο Ρ Ο Ѳ Ε Ο Σ Δ̅ōρόθεος), and Oltos has added a comment: Ι Σ Ι ϱ Σ Ο Η Ǝ Μ V Ο V Α Η h̅αλούμενονος εῖσι ('he is about to jump'). Between the two athletes a pipe-player called Smikythos (Σ Μ Ι Κ V Σμίκν[θος]) provides the rhythm for their movements. On the other side of the vase are a discus-thrower called Antiphanes (Α Ν Τ Ι Φ Α Ν Ε Ɔ Ἀντιφάνἒς) and his trainer (Σ Ǝ · ꓩ · ꓤ · Α, perhaps Ἀντιμένἒς, Antimenes), as well as another trainer (Α Ʌ Κ Ε Τ Ε Σ Ἀλκέτἒς, Alketes), and a boy victor, Epainetos, who is praised for his beauty (Ἐπαίνετος καλός, 'Epainetos is fair'). A judge called Kleainetos (Κ Ʌ Ε Α Ι Ν Ε Τ Ο Ϛ Κλεαίνετος) is just visible on the right in the frontispiece.

Some of the inscriptions run from right to left because they start near the person to whom they refer. Oltos adds two comments in which the vase itself addresses the viewer: ρ ◻ Μ Ε (πô με, 'drink me') and Ο · ꓲ Σ Α Χ (χάσκō, 'I open my mouth wide').

42   Signature of Tleson the potter, c. 550 BC. BM GR 1867.5–8.946.

43 Amphora signed by Exekias as potter, *c.* 540–530 BC. BM GR 1836.2–24.127.

44 Wedding-reception of Peleus and Thetis on a bowl signed by Sophilos as potter, *c.* 580 BC. BM GR 1971.11–1.1.

An important series of vases are those made to contain the olive oil given as prizes in the Panathenaic Games at Athens. One side shows the event in which the prize was won, the other shows the goddess Athena, whose birthday the festival celebrated, and bears the inscription τὸν Ἀθέ̄νεθεν ἄθλōν ('(one) of the prizes from Athens'). On an example in New York the painter did not allow quite enough space for the inscription.

The black-figure technique of vase-painting survived on Panathenaic prize amphorae long after red-figure was invented (and even after it was eventually abandoned) because it was traditional. During the fourth century BC the name of the Archon is often added, and the inscriptions instead of being written sideways down the vase are written in a vertical column, like the 'down' lights in a crossword puzzle. An example in London, commissioned in the archonship of Pythodelos (336/5), retains the Attic alphabet for the traditional prize formula but employs Ionic forms including *eta* and *omega* in the Archon inscription Πνθόδηλος ἄρχων.

A black-figured amphora in New York has a puzzling inscription that seems to have no connection with the painted decoration, a warrior wearing greaves and

45   Prize amphora from the Panathenaic games, *c.* 530 BC. MMA 56.171.4.

46   Inscriptions from a Panathenaic prize-amphora, 336/5 BC. BM GR 1873.8–20.371.

carrying a helmet, spear and shield. The first problem is to decide whether the second and third *epsilons* should be read as 'short' or 'long' (that is, standing for *eta*). If short, the text would read ὃυ' ὀβέλō καὶ μ' ἔθιγες ('Two obols and you touch me', that is, 'You can have me for two obols'). In general scholars prefer to read ὃυ' ὀβέλō καὶ μὲ̄ θίγε̄ς ('Two obols – and hands off', that is, 'Do not touch: I am worth more than two obols'). The inscription may well be a joke by the vase-painter. It is actually written from right to left.

The inscription on a bronze statuette in New York, originally dedicated as a votive offering, is in an early form of the Attic alphabet, but relatively easy to interpret. The statuette is of a lyre-player, barely 8 cm high, with an inscription on the back of his tunic: Δόλιχος μ' ἀνέθε̄κεν ('Dolichos dedicated me'). The letters include an early form of *chi* (+) and a very unusual *sigma* with no fewer than five bars. *Theta* is written simply as a circle with a dot in it, and the lowest bar of *epsilon* is placed high on the stem, giving the letter a tail rather like our F.

Of the alphabets used in other parts of Greece during the archaic period the Ionic

48

47   *Above* Amphora with a price-inscription, *c.* 540 BC. MMA 56.171.13.

48   *Right*   Bronze statuette of a lyre-player, *c.* 500 BC. MMA 08.258.5.

49 Bowl dedicated by Sostratos to Aphrodite at Naukratis, *c.* 600–500 BC.
BM GR 1888.6–1.456.

50 Dedication by Rhoikos to Aphrodite at Naukratis, *c.* 600–550 BC. BM GR 1888.6–1.392.

is perhaps the easiest for the modern reader since the characters are close in shape to those in use today. A bowl from Naucratis in Egypt has a votive inscription incised inside the rim: Σώστρατος μ' ἀνέ[θ]ηκεν τῆ' φροδίτηι ('Sostratos dedicated me to Aphrodite'). The 'long' vowels *eta* (already in the open form H) and *omega* (Ω) are distinguished from the 'short' *epsilon* (E) and *omicron* (O), and *sigma* is of the familiar four-barred type.

Another vase from Naucratis with a *graffito* ('incised inscription') was dedicated to Aphrodite by a man from Samos: 'Ροῖρος μ' ἀνέθηκε τ[ῆι Ἀφρ]οδίτηι ('Rhoikos dedicated me to Aphrodite'). It has been suggested that the dedicator may be identified with Rhoikos of Samos, an early sculptor credited with the invention of casting bronze statues. Rhoikos spells his name not with *kappa* (K) but with the guttural *qoppa* (9), a character that was widespread in early alphabets but gradually fell out of use in the sixth century BC. The form of the initial *rho* without a leg is typical of the Samian alphabet.

A different form of *rho* with a tail (R), which as we have seen was transmitted to the west by the Euboeans, is also found in most of the local alphabets of the Greek mainland. A bronze spear-butt in New York appears to have been part of the spoils of a battle dedicated by the victors to Castor and Polydeuces: ἱερὸς Τυνδαρίδαινς ἀπ' Ἐραέōν ('Sacred to the Tyndaridai from the Heraeans'). Although the *sigma* is of the four-barred type that we have seen in Ionic script, separate forms for *eta* and *omega* are lacking in Arcadian. The case-ending for the dative form 'to the Tyndaridai' is characteristic of the Arcadian dialect.

51 Bronze spear-butt dedicated to the Dioscuri, *c.* 500–480 BC. MMA 38.11.7.

The tailed *rho* is prominent in the dedicatory inscription on another item of spoil, a bronze helmet found at Olympia in 1817: hιάρον ὁ Δεινομένεος | καὶ τοὶ Συρακόσιοι | τᾶι Δὶ Τυράν⟨ōν⟩ ἀπὸ Κύμας. ('Hieron (son) of Deinomenes and the Syracusans (dedicated me) to Zeus, Etruscan (spoils) from Cumae'). Hieron's victory over the Etruscans in a naval battle off Cumae in 474 BC is recorded by the historian Diodorus, so this inscription is quite closely dated. It is one of several by Hieron and his brother Gelon that provide evidence for the Syracusan alphabet during this period. Another typical feature is the late survival of the closed form of *heta* (Ⴞ) as an aspirate. The origin of the alphabets used by Syracuse and other Doric colonies in Sicily is not fully understood. Syracuse itself was a colony of Corinth but does not use the Corinthian alphabet, perhaps because when the first Syracusan colonists left Corinth the alphabet was not yet in use there.

56

52   Etruscan bronze helmet dedicated by the Syracusans to Zeus at Olympia, 474 BC.
BM GR 1823.6–10.1.

Although it shares the tailed *rho* and the closed form of the aspirate (Ө), the alphabet used in Argos is not closely connected to the Syracusan. In its earliest form Argive has much in common with Corinthian, including the use of the sibilant *san*. Around 500 BC, however, *san* in Argive gave way to the four-barred *sigma* seen on a

53   prize hydria of about 470–60 BC, together with a distinctive form of *lamda* (Ⱶ): πὰρ hέρας ⋮ Ἀργείας ⋮ haϝέθλδν ('(One) of the prizes from Argive Hera'). The most famous prizes from Argos were the bronze shields mentioned by an ancient commentator on the poet Pindar, one of which appears on the Rhamnousian relief, but bronze vessels like bowls and hydriai were also given as prizes, as inscriptions like this one show.

The Argive dialect was one of those that long retained a sound similar to the Semitic *waw* and represented by (Ϝ), usually called *digamma* because it resembles two *gammas*, one above the other. Here it appears near the beginning of 'prizes', separating the *alpha* and *epsilon*. The prize inscriptions on Attic Panathenaic amphorae show that this sound had already disappeared from the Attic dialect.

Prizes were awarded not only for athletic successes. Around 540–30 BC a young

54   woman called Melousa, who lived in Taras (modern Taranto in the 'heel' of Italy), won a prize for her skill in working wool, a splendid black-figured cup imported from Athens. Her success was recorded in a *graffito* underneath the foot: Μελόσας · ἐμὶ · νικατέριον · ξαίνοσα τὰς κόρας ἐνίκε ('I am Melousa's prize; she won the maidens' carding contest'). The cup, now in New York, is said to have been found in Taranto, and this is confirmed by the use of Laconian letter-forms, including Χ for *xi*. The dialect is Doric, with *alpha* in νικατέριον where other dialects including Attic would have *eta*.

53   Bronze prize-hydria from the games at Argos, *c.* 470–460 BC. MMA 26.50.

54   Melousa's prize for her skill in wool-carding, *c.* 540–530 BC. MMA 44.11.1.

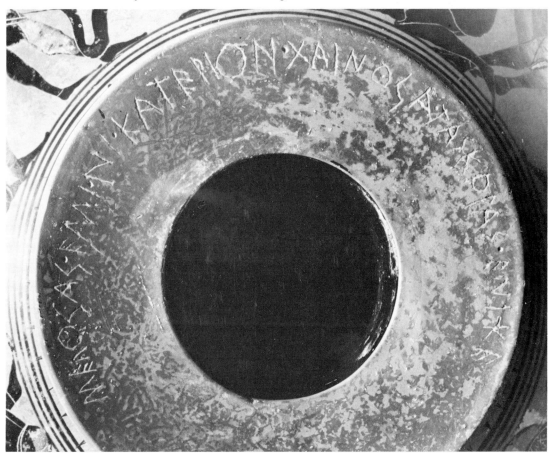

55 Aineta's aryballos, with her portrait and the names of her lovers, *c.* 625 BC. Reproduced over actual size. BM GR 1865.12–13.1.

55 The same Doric pronunciation is reflected in the spelling of the names on a Corinthian *aryballos* ('perfume-pot') that once belonged to Aineta: Ἀινέτα | ἐμί. | Μενέας | Θέρōν ‖ Μυρμίδας | Εὔδιϙος | Λυσανδρίδας | Χαρικλίδας | Δεξίλος ‖ Ξένϝōν | Φρύξ. ('I am Aineta (*or* Aineta's). Meneas, Theron, Myrmides, Eudikos, Lysandrides, Chariklides, Dexilos, Xenon, Phryx').

The inscription ought to be easy to read since it consists almost entirely of personal names in the nominative, presumably a list of Aineta's lovers. It is made more difficult not so much by the Doric spelling as by the use of the archaic Corinthian alphabet, in which several characters resemble those alloted to different letters in other alphabets. So ß is not *beta* but *epsilon*, and Ʂ is *iota*, not *sigma*. *Sigma* in fact, does not exist in the Corinthian alphabet, which uses *san* (M) as the sibilant: this in turn must be distinguished from *mu*, written M. The use of *qoppa* and the presence of *digamma* should by now cause no more difficulty than the absence of the 'long' vowels *eta* and *omega*. Experts have disagreed since the nineteenth century whether Ἀινέτα is the nominative form of the name or a Doric genitive, that is, whether the 'portrait' is saying 'I am Aineta' or the pot itself, like many others, is announcing ownership: 'I belong to Aineta.'

A plate from Kamiros in Rhodes is hardly more difficult to read than Aineta's 56 *aryballos* but poses problems of its own. It shows an episode from the *Iliad* (17.59–113), with Menelaus (Μενέλας) and Hector (Ἕκτōρ) fighting over the body of Euphorbos (Εὔφορβος). Hector's name is written retrograde, and the *rho* has no tail. Menelaus (here 'Menelas') again exemplifies the difference between *mu* at the beginning and *san* at the end, and has *lamda* in the Argive form (Ⱶ) that we saw on the bronze hydria. The *beta* in Euphorbos, however, is of the normal type, not the idiosyncratic Argive form (Ϻ). Since the plate itself is East Greek, that is, was made in one of the Greek settlements in the eastern Aegean, on the coast of Asia Minor or on one of the offshore islands, it implies that a modified version of the Argive alphabet was in use in one of the Doric-speaking cities on or near Rhodes. Kalymna has been suggested.

56   Plate showing the death of Euphorbos, *c.* 600 BC. BM GR 1860.4–4.1.

An island at the other end of the Greek world, Kephallenia off the north-western coast of Greece, is the likely source of a bronze discus dedicated to the Dioscuri:

57

Ἐχσοΐδα μ᾽ ἀνέθέκε Διϝὸς ϙόροιν μεγάλοιο ⋮
χάλκεον ℎōι νίκασε Κεφαλᾶνας μεγαθύμος.

Exoidas dedicated me to the sons of mighty Zeus, (the) bronze with which he overcame the great-hearted Kephallenians.

The inscription consists of two lines of verse, Homeric in metre and diction: the last two words are quoted from the *Iliad*, and the end of the first line is adapted from the 'Homeric Hymn to the Dioscuri' with only the case-ending of 'sons' changed. It is written retrograde in a single spiral line that begins around the circumference of the discus. The alphabet, like others in the west, belongs to the 'red' group, with Ѱ for *chi*; it uses *san* (M) rather than *sigma* as the sibilant, and has *qoppa* as well as *kappa*. The aspirate is the normal closed form (日), but *gamma* is of an unusual lunate form found also on nearby Ithaka.

A similar 'red' alphabet, related also to Arcadian and Laconian, was in use at Olympia, where a bronze tablet recording an alliance between the people of Elis and the Heraeans was found in 1813. Similar inscriptions have been found at Olympia more recently. All the tablets have holes so that they could be nailed up, probably in a temple.

58

57   Bronze discus dedicated to the Dioscuri, *c.* 550–525. BM GR 1898.7-16.3.

ἁ ϝράτρα τοῖρ Ϝαλείοις : καὶ τοῖς Ἐρ|ϝαōοις : συνμαχία κ᾿ ἔα ἑκατὸν
ϝέτεα : | ἄρχοι δέ κα τοΐ : αἰ δέ τι δέοι : αἴτε ϝέπος αἴτε ϝ|άργον : συνέαν
κ᾿ ἀλάλοις : τά τ᾿ ἄλ⟨α⟩ καὶ πὰ|ρ πολέμω : αἰ δὲ μὰ συνέαν : τάλαντόν κ᾿|
ἀργύρω : ἀποτίνοιαν : τōι Δὶ Ὀλυνπίōι : τοὶ κα|δαλέμενοι : λατρειόμενον :
αἰ δέ τιρ τὰ γ|ράφεα : ται᾿ καδαλέοιτο : αἴτε ϝέτας αἴτε τ|ελεστὰ : αἴτε
δᾶμος : ἔν τἐπιάρōι κ᾿ ἐνέχ‖οιτο τōι ᾿νταῦτ᾿ ἐγραμένōι.

The treaty between the Eleans and the Heraeans: let there be an alliance for 100
years; and let this (year) begin (it); and if there be any need, either of word or of
deed, let them stand by each other in other matters and in war; but if they do not
stand by (each other), let the defaulters pay to Olympian Zeus a talent of silver for
his service; and if anyone damages this inscription, whether private citizen or
magistrate or community, let him be liable to the sacred penalty written herein.

The inscription is probably to be dated around 500 BC. In addition to the use of
digamma features of the local dialect include 'rhotacism', that is, the substitution of
rho for *sigma*, for example, at the end of the third word, and the pronunciation
αι instead of *ει* for 'if'.

This inscription was bequeathed to the British Museum by Richard Payne Knight
(1750–1824), a wealthy landowner and antiquary, who was also a distinguished
amateur scholar. His attempt to transcribe the text into the common Greek dialect
and script of the Roman period was remarkably successful. He took account of
digamma, recognised the 'red' Ψ as *chi*, and correctly interpreted various features of
the dialect including rhotacism. His failure to recognise *τοΐ* as the dialect form of
τόδε ('this') is entirely understandable, given the state of knowledge of Greek dialects
in the early nineteenth century. His modest disclaimer of total certainty might well be
taken as a motto by modern epigraphers: *Judicent tamen doctiores, et siquid
probabilius habuerint, proferant* ('Let the more learned sit in judgement, and if they
have a more probable (reading), propose it').

58   Treaty between the Eleans and the Heraeans, *c.* 500 BC. BM GR 1824.4–99.17.

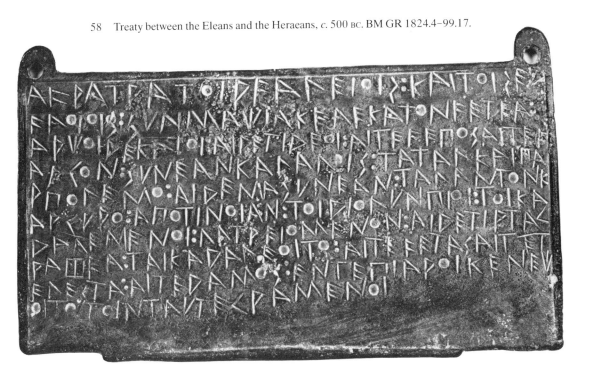

Further Reading

A. G. Woodhead, *The Study of Greek Inscriptions* (1959): the indispensable textbook.
Sterling Dow, *Conventions in Editing (Greek, Roman and Byzantine Scholarly Aids* 2, 1969): essential reading for professional epigraphers.
R. Meiggs and D. Lewis (eds), *A Selection of Greek Historical Inscriptions to the End of the Fifth Century BC* (1969), abbr. Meiggs and Lewis, updates and largely replaces:
M. N. Tod, *A Selection of Greek Historical Inscriptions to the End of the Fifth Century BC* (2nd edn, 1946), abbr. Tod i².
id., A Selection of Greek Historical Inscriptions, Vol. II from 403 to 328 BC (1949), abbr. Tod ii.
L. H. Jeffery, *The Local Scripts of Archaic Greece* (1961: new impression forthcoming), abbr. *LSAG*, a monumental study of the early Greek alphabets: not for beginners.
R. Meiggs, *The Athenian Empire* (1972), makes much use of epigraphic evidence.
Alan E. Samuel, *Greek and Roman Chronology* (1972), is invaluable for ancient calendars.

Abbreviations and References

Museum Catalogues

BM Cat. Bronzes	H. B. Walters, *Catalogue of the Bronzes, Greek, Roman and Etruscan in the Department of Greek and Roman Antiquities, British Museum* (1899)
BM Cat. Sculpture i, iii	A. H. Smith, *A Catalogue of Sculpture in the Department of Greek and Roman Antiquities, British Museum*, Vols i and iii (1892, 1904)
BM Cat. Sculpture i, 1	F. N. Pryce, *Catalogue of Sculpture in the Department of Greek and Roman Antiquities, British Museum*, Vol. i, part 1, *Prehellenic and Early Greek* (1928)
BM Cat. Vases	H. B. Walters, *Catalogue of the Greek and Etruscan Vases in the British Museum*, Vol. ii *Black-figured Vases* (1893)
MMA Cat. Bronzes	G. M. A. Richter, *The Metropolitan Museum of Art: Greek, Etruscan and Roman Bronzes* (1915)
MMA Cat. Sculpture	G. M. A. Richter, *Catalogue of Greek Sculptures in The Metropolitan Museum of Art* (1954)

Epigraphic Publications

CIG	*Corpus Inscriptionum Graecarum* (4 vols 1828–77)
GIBM	*The Collection of Ancient Greek Inscriptions in the British Museum* (4 vols 1874–1916)
IG	*Inscriptiones Graecae* (many vols 1873–)
SEG	*Supplementum Epigraphicum Graecum* (serial publication, i, 1923–)

References

Cover BM GR 1867.5-8.117. *BM Cat. Sculpture* i, 809. *CIG* 2429. *GIBM* 365.

1 MMA 10.210.18. Beazley, J. D., *Attic Red-figure Vase-painters*, 2nd edn (1963), p. 54, no. 7.
2 The precinct of the Eponymous Heroes at Athens. *The Athenian Agora: A Guide* (1976), p. 69, fig. 26.
3 BM GR 1863.5-16.1. *IG* i³.264, 272. Meritt, B. D., Wade-Gery, H. T., and McGregor, M. F., *The Athenian Tribute Lists* i (1939), pp. 3 and 33-4, no. 60, figs 38-9, pls VII, xv.

4 MMA 24.97.21. Jeffery, L. H., *LSAG*, p. 241, no. 22, pl. 48.
5 BM GR 1816.6-10.206. *GIBM* 5. *IG* i³.53. Meiggs and Lewis, pp. 171-5, no. 63.
6 BM GR 1805.7-3.183. *BM Cat. Sculpture* i, 628. *GIBM* 123. *IG* ii².12332.
7 BM GR 1970.9-25.1. *IG* xii.2, 129. Cook, B. F., *Antiquaries Journal* li (1971), pp. 263-6, pls XLIII(b) and XLV.
8 BM GR 1872.4-5.19. *BM Cat. Sculpture* B 16. *GIBM* 518. Tod i², pp. 9-10, no. 6.

9 MMA 11.185. *MMA Cat. Sculpture* 15. *IG* i². 981. Guarducci, M., in Richter, G. M. A., *The Archaic Gravestones of Attica* (1961), pp. 159–65, no. 37. Jeffery, L. H., *LSAG* p. 78, no. 32, pl. 4. *Id., Annual of the British School at Athens* lxvii (1962), pp. 146–7, no. 63, pl. 41a. Clairmont, C. W., *Gravestone and Epigram* (1970), pp. 13–15, no. 1, pl. 1.

10 MMA 59.11.19. *CIG* 234. *IG* ii².3145. *SEG* xxi.698. Bother, D. von, *Metropolitan Museum of Art Bulletin* n.s. xix (1960/1), pp. 181–3, fig. 1. Robert, J. and L., *Revue des Etudes Grecques* lxxiii (1960), p. 157, no. 144; lxxvi (1963), p. 132, no. 80.

11 BM GR 1850.7–24.1. *BM Cat. Sculpture* i, 599. *GIBM* 86. *IG* i².6338.

12 BM GR 1870.3–20.88 *CIG* 2904. *GIBM* 399. Hiller von Gaertringen, F., *Inschriften von Priene* (1906), p. 129, no. 156. Tod ii, pp. 241–2, no. 184.

13 BM GR 1872.6–10.43. *GIBM* 443.

14 BM GR 1877.5–11.1. *GIBM* 171.

15 BM GR 1970.6–2.1. *CIG* 5763. *IG* xiv.617. Cook, B. F., *Antiquaries Journal* li (1971), pp. 260–3, pls XLIII(a) and XLIV. To the references there cited add: F. Poulsen in *Photographische Einzelaufnahmen antiker Sculpturen* (ed. P. Arndt and G. Lippold), xi (1929), p. 25, no. 3098.

16 BM GR 1805.7–3.232. *GIBM* 44. *IG* ii².2191.

17 BM GR 1772.7–3.2. *BM Cat. Sculpture* i, 703. *CIG* 3256. *GIBM* 1024.

18 BM GR 1948.10–19.1. Haynes, D. E. L., and Tod, M.N., *Journal of Hellenic Studies* lxxiii (1953), pp. 138–40, pl. v. *SEG* xii.561.

19 BM GR 1805.7–3.211. *BM Cat. Sculpture* iii, 2391. *GIBM* 1114. *IG* xiv.2131.

20 BM GR 1805.7–3.187. *BM Cat. Sculpture* i, 649. *CIG* 6866. *GIBM* 1127.

21 BM GR 1859.12–26.19. *GIBM* 928.

22 BM GR 1847.12–20.3. *CIG* 2664. *GIBM* 918.

23 BM GR 1864.3–31.6. *GIBM* 175.

24 BM GR 1785.5–27.9. *GIBM* 13. *IG* ii².2498. *SEG* xxxii.226.

25 BM GR 1816.6–10.348. *GIBM* 37. *IG* i².945. *SEG* x.414, xxi.125, xxii.64. Tod i², pp. 127–8, no. 59. P. A. Hansen, *Carmina epigraphica saeculorum VIII–V a.Chr.n.* (1983), pp. 8–10, no. 10.

26 BM GR 1816.6–10.173. *GIBM* 38. *IG* i².949.

27 BM GR 1816.6–10.282. *GIBM* 26. *IG* i³.309–10.

28 BM GR 1785.5–27.1. *GIBM* 35. *IG* i³.474.

29 MMA 16.174.6. *MMA Cat. Sculpture* 14. *SEG* iii.55. Guarducci, M., in Richter, G. M. A., *The Archaic Grayestones of Attica* (1961), p. 156, no. 34. Jeffery, L. H., *LSAG*, p. 77, no. 20, pl. 3. *Id., Annual of the British School at Athens* lxvii (1962), p. 118, no. 2, pl. 32(c).

30 MMA 15.167. *MMA Cat. Sculpture* 20. *SEG* x.460. Guarducci, M. in Richter, G. M. A., *The Archaic Gravestones of Attica* (1961), pp. 169–70, no. 61. Jeffery, L. H., *LSAG*, p. 78, no. 34, pl. 4. *Id., Annual of the British School at Athens* lxvii (1962), p. 147, no. 65, pl. 41(b).

31 BM GR 1785.5–27.2. *GIBM* 1. *IG* i³.244.

32 BM GR 1816.6–10.107. *GIBM* 1002. *SEG* iv.667. Guarducci, M. in Richter, G.M.A., *The Archaic Gravestones of Attica* (1961), pp. 165–8, no. 53. Jeffery, L. H., *LSAG*, p. 371, nos 43–4, pl. 71.

33 BM GR 1867.11–22.441. *GIBM* 678. Jeffery, L. H., *LSAG*, p. 344, no. 55(a).

34 BM GR 1816.6–10.377. *GIBM* 158. *IG* vii. 3171.

35 BM GR 1856.8–26.6. *GIBM* 245. Segre, M., *Tituli Calymnii (Annuario della Scuola Archeologica di Atene* n.s. v–vii [1944–5]), p. 43, no. 1, pl. VII.

36 *BM EA* 24. *GIBM* 1065. Andrews, C., *The Rosetta Stone* (1981).

37 BM GR 1816.6–24.38. British Museum, *A Guide to the Exhibition Illustrating Greek and Roman Life*, 2nd edn (1920), p. 205.

38 BM GR 1925.7–20.1. Previously unpublished.

39 BM GR 1873.8–20.129. *BM Cat. Bronzes* 331. *IG* ii². 1849. Kroll, J., *Athenian Bronze Allotment Plates* (1972), pp. 183–4, no. 83.

40 MMA 90.9.29. B. F. Cook, *Inscribed Hadra Vases in The Metropolitan Museum of Art* (1966), p. 24, no. 9, pls III and XI.

41 BM GR 1906.10–20.2. British Museum, *A Guide to the Exhibition Illustrating Greek and Roman Life*, 2nd edn (1920), p. 198.

42 BM GR 1867.5–8.946. *BM Cat. Vases* B 421. *CIG* 8301. Beazley, J. D., *Attic Black-figure Vase-painters* (1956), p. 181, no. 1.

43 BM GR 1836.2–24.127. *BM Cat. Vases* B 210. Beazley, J.D., *Attic Black-figure Vase-painters* (1956), p. 144, no. 7.

44 BM GR 1971.11–1.1. Williams, D., J. Paul Getty Museum, *Occasional Papers on Antiquities* i (1983), pp. 9–34.

45 MMA 56.171.4. Beazley, J. D., *Paralipomena* (1971), p. 127, no. 1.

46 BM GR 1873.8–20.371. *BM Cat. Vases* B 607. Beazley, J. D., *Attic Black-figure Vase-painters* (1956), p. 415, no. 4.

47 MMA 56.171.13. Beazley, J. D., *Paralipomena* (1971), p. 55, no. 50. Webster, T. B. L., *Potter and Patron in Classical Athens* (1972), pl. 77–8, pl. 10.

48 MMA 08.258.5. *MMA Cat. Bronzes* 59. Richter, G. M. A., *Handbook of the Greek Collection* (1953), p. 67, pl. 48c.

49 BM GR 1888.6–1.456. Gardner, E. A., *Naukratis* ii (1888), p. 62, no. 701, pls VI and XXI.

50 BM GR 1888.6–1.392. Gardner, E.A., *Naukratis* ii (1888), p. 65, no. 778, pls VII and XXI. Jeffery, L. H., *LSAG*, p. 341, no. 3(b).

51 MMA 38.11.7. *SEG* xi.1045. Jeffery, L. H., *LSAG*, p. 215, no. 11, pl. 40.

52 BM GR 1823.6–10.1. *BM Cat. Bronzes* 250. *GIBM* 1155. *SEG* xi.1206. Jeffery, L. H., *LSAG*, p. 275, no. 7, pl. 51. Meiggs and Lewis, p. 62, no. 29.

53 MMA 26.50. *SEG* xi.355. Jeffery, L. H., *LSAG*, p. 169, no. 16, pl. 29.

54 MMA 44.11.1. Jeffery, L.H., *LSAG*, p. 283, no. 1, pl. 53.

55 BM GR 1865.12–13.1. *IG* iv.348. Jeffery, L. H., *LSAG*, p. 131, no. 9, pl. 19. Guarducci, M., *Epigrafia Greca* iii (1974), p. 462, fig. 181.

56 BM GR 1860.4–4.1. Jeffery, L. H., *LSAG*, p. 358, no. 47, pl. 69.

57 BM GR 1898.7–16.3. *BM Cat. Bronzes* 3207. *GIBM* 952. *IG* xi.1.649. *SEG* xiv.470. Jeffery, L. H., *LSAG*, p. 234, no. 5, pl. 45.

58 BM GR 1824.4–99.17. *BM Cat. Bronzes* 264. *GIBM* 157. *SEG* xi.1182. Jeffery, L. H., *LSAG*, p. 220, no. 6, pl. 42. Meiggs and Lewis, pp. 31–3, no. 17.

Index

Figure numbers are in italic type.